LETTERS *from the* BATTLEFIELD

Edited by Glyn Harper

NEW ZEALAND SOLDIERS WRITE HOME • 1914-18

HarperCollins*Publishers (New Zealand) Limited*

The publishers and the author wish to thank *Sunday Star-Times* for their cooperation with this publication.

First published 2001

HarperCollins*Publishers (New Zealand) Limited*
P.O. Box 1, Auckland

ISBN 1 86950 379 1

Front cover photo: William, George and John Malcolm
courtesy of Lindsay Malcolm
Back cover photo: Kippenberger Military Archive and Research
Library, Army Museum, Waiouru: H474

Text set in Palatino and Electra; display in Iris
Designed and typeset by Chris O'Brien
Printed by Brebner Print, Auckland

To the fallen

Contents

Photo credits

Alexander Turnbull Library: page 46, PAColl-2667-002; page 67, 1/2-012773; G; page 69, Eph-POSTCARD-WWI-01; page 72, 1/1-002085; page 112, 1/2-013108; G; page 161, PAColl-2667-001.

Kippenberger Military Archive and Research Library, Army Museum, Waiouru, New Zealand: page 20, 1992.774; page 81, 2000.979; page 84, 2000.978; page 106, H474; page 128, H467.

Individual families: pages 25 and 63, Pamela Cotton; pages 36 and 157, Paul Christophers; page 40, Ian Harvey; page 45, Lauretta Eades; page 53, Maree Barham; page 57, Margaret Dempsey; page 65, Jim Connor; page 78, Maryrose Bell; page 87, P.M. Kay; page 96, Roland Sarten; page 98, Derek Newman; page 103, Cyril McKeefry; page 107, Dora May Sutcliffe; page 109, Gay Dowling; page 114, G.W. Stanbridge; page 116, Sally Duggan; page 123, Ross McMillan; page 132, Stephanie Grieve; page 136, Patricia Warnock; page 139, Aynsley Taylor; page 144, Marian Young; page 145, Lindsay Malcolm; page 149, Alan Hughes; page 159, William and Elizabeth Eaddy.

Acknowledgements

The publication of this collection of letters would not have been possible if various individuals and families had not made them available. To those people who sent in their letters to the *Sunday Star Times*, who deposited them at the Alexander Turnbull Library or the Kippenberger Military Archive, or who sent their letters directly to me, you have my sincere gratitude. You should take some comfort from knowing that you have preserved a small slice of New Zealand family history.

I am indebted to the staff of the two research institutions mentioned above. The staff at the Alexander Turnbull Library never cease to amaze me with their patience, dedication and kindness. They could not be more helpful. The same is equally true of Dolores Ho and Windsor Jones of the Kippenberger Military Archive in Waiouru.

Paul Lumsden from Nelson designed the excellent maps.

Once again I wish to thank Ian Watt and Sue Page of HarperCollins publishers for their encouragement and support. This is our third venture together and I hope there will be many more to follow.

Finally, I wish to acknowledge the support of my two daughters Natalie and Rhiannon. Checking old letters against typescript and compiling an index might not sound like much of a family bonding experience, but we found it so.

Publisher's Note

The letters in this collection come from a number of contributors, each with differing literary styles and levels of education. In addition, many of the letters would have been written under the most trying of conditions. In order to enhance readability for a modern audience, small editorial changes have been necessary. For the main part this has involved the introduction of punctuation. Abbreviations have been spelled out in full, ampersands replaced with 'and', capitalisation has been reduced, and spelling has been corrected, but only where the author's original meaning was absolutely clear. Letters are not necessarily reproduced in full; omitted material is indicated by an ellipsis. Occasionally, an editorial explanation has been added to the letter; this appears in square brackets.

Introduction:
The First World War and New Zealand

In the history of the twentieth century, the First World War, or 'The Great War' as it is still called, can be regarded as 'the most important and far-reaching political and military event of the century'.[1] The reasons for this are clear. For the first time in history a war touched the lives of millions of people across the globe. It brought Americans, Australians, Canadians, Africans, Asians and New Zealanders to parts of the world they otherwise would never have seen. Very few New Zealanders at the turn of the century even knew where Gallipoli was and the thought of going there, if given the opportunity, would never have crossed their minds. Few New Zealanders, too, would have ever made their way to the Middle East, Northern France or Belgium but for the war of 1914–18. This war brought New Zealand soldiers, and many others like them, to these places in their thousands. The First World War then was truly an 'international story with unprecedented sweep'.[2] It changed the lives of millions of people on a scale never witnessed before and New Zealand, despite its isolation, was caught up in the whirlwind.

The First World War had important implications for people living in the twentieth century. Most of these people have unknowingly lived in the shadow of this war all their lives. At its most general level, the war of 1914–18 set the pattern of international relations that has persisted since its ending more than eighty years ago. One of the unexpected consequences of the First World War — and wars always have unexpected consequences — was the creation of a world order we now take for granted. This has included the division of the world in to East and West in a 'Cold War' which persisted until the last decade of the twentieth century. The war of 1914–18 also saw the emergence of the USA as a dominant, although initially reluctant, world power, a

11

nation standing 'on the brink of global economic supremacy' to use the words of Niall Ferguson.[3] In tandem with this development was the decline of both the United Kingdom and France as world powers. Yet another consequence was the creation of new nation states from the wreck of the Austro-Hungarian and Turkish Empires, a problematical process that continues to unravel to this day.

The First World War also established a general trend of the twentieth century in that it was a triumph of liberal democracy over monarchism. In May 1914, German Chancellor Theobald von Bethman Hollweg had warned that a major war 'would topple many a throne'. He was right. The war that came three months later killed off three major European monarchies and severely damaged many more. In their place, republics were established, most of them democratically elected, which was 'a triumph of republicanism undreamt of even in the 1790s'.[4]

While few New Zealanders like to acknowledge it, war and the military service it entails has played an important role in the shaping of the nation. This is especially true of New Zealand's experience in the twentieth century, a century that began and ended with New Zealand committing large numbers of its armed forces to military operations far away from the country's shores. Such a record of service, together with the introduction of compulsory military service at various times throughout the century, has meant that the single greatest shared experience of New Zealand males in the last hundred years has been service in the military. Nowhere is this trend more clearly established than in New Zealand's contribution to the war of 1914–18.

In most combatant nations, about 50 per cent of the male population between 18 and 45 years of age joined up. This participation rate in a war by so many nations was unprecedented. It also meant that the total casualties and losses as a proportion of those who served would surpass any previous war experience. New Zealand's contribution to the 1914–18 war effort has been described by one of the leading historians of the Great War as being 'second to none'.[5] By the end of the war New Zealand had sent 19.4 per cent of her men to the war, compared to 13.5 per cent for Australia and Canada. From a population base of just on a million people, more than 10 per cent of the population, 117,175 New Zealanders, served in the armed forces during the war and 102,438 embarked for overseas service. This was a truly staggering effort. As a proportion of its population, the New Zealand casualty rate was the highest of all the British Dominions.[6] The tragic cost of this war is still evident today. It has been engraved on the New Zealand landscape where towns, cities and communities have erected their monuments to the dead of the First World War.

The casualties of the First World War, though, were not limited to the dead and wounded. They also included those men who returned, many of whom seemed unaffected by what they had seen and done. In truth, most of the men who returned from this war were casualties and had to live with their war memories for the rest of their lives. For many, the war actually came to dominate their lives. As one participant in the Passchendaele battles told Lyn Macdonald: 'In a way, I lived my whole life between the ages of nineteen and twenty-three. Everything that happened after that was almost an anti-climax'.[7]

The immediate impact of the war was on the private lives of those affected by it. It should never be forgotten that, no matter how mechanical it might appear, war is above all a human activity. Therefore, the First World War meant that world history had become family history. This is because, to use the words of Jay Winter and Blaine Baggett, 'War is always the destroyer of families and the Great War was to date the greatest destroyer of them all.'[8] For New Zealanders, while they lived thousand of miles from the scene of the conflict, this war affected their lives like no other. If not by the end of the Gallipoli campaign, then certainly by the end of the attacks at Passchendaele two years later, nearly every New Zealand family had experienced the cost of war first-hand. Modern warfare had perfected the art of killing *en masse* and this meant universal suffering and bereavement for all nations involved in the conflict. New Zealand's share of this suffering was immense and out of all proportion to her tiny size. With scarcely a New Zealand family left untouched by the death or injury of someone dear to them, the war affected all levels of New Zealand society like no other tragedy.

Neither did the war end in 1918 for those families caught up in this deadly struggle. For those left to rebuild their lives after the conflict the family would be defined by those now missing from it and by those scarred, perhaps permanently, by their experiences of the conflict. Families were very different after the war. The war had interrupted enterprises begun, projects initiated, unions contemplated and ideas expressed, and many of these could not be recovered. The war was a huge chasm between a paradise imagined and the reality that was.

The legacy of the war, with its destruction, horror and suffering, was overwhelming and irreversible.

This cost was not anticipated in 1914. Totally unaware of what lay ahead, New Zealand's entry into the war was somewhat light-hearted and carefree, prompting the historian Christopher Pugsley to remark that 1914 'was more like the start of an international tour by an All Black team rather than soldiers embarking for war'.[9] For the participants, the war proved to be far from 'the great adventure' they had anticipated. This naïve and innocent spirit would be shattered by the horrors and suffering of the long war that followed. Never again would New Zealand commit its soldiers to war in the same spirit or manner.

By the end of the war New Zealand had been transformed and was in 1920 very different from what it had been in 1914. The old certainties that had anchored people in 1914 were now eroded or had vanished entirely. This included such ideals as the conviction that war reinvigorated nations, created character, was manly, glorious and that a relatively bloodless victory was possible. Notions of duty, honour, sacrifice and Empire all suffered too. Before the war, the United Kingdom had set the standard for what was good and pure, the things to which a nation aspired, and New Zealanders had tried to mirror themselves on the 'British' model. As a result of the First World War, though, New Zealanders realised, especially through the returning soldiers, that New Zealand and New Zealanders were different and this difference did not imply inferiority. New Zealand nationalism and a sense of identity had been born. If, as has been alleged, the war made Australia 'a nation at last', it had certainly begun, but by no means completed, this process for New Zealand.[10]

This book is a collection of letters written by New Zealand soldiers of the First World War. Most of the letters were sent to the *Sunday Star Times* newspaper as the result of a feature article for Anzac Day in 1999. As with most historical sources, letters can be unreliable if they are used solely by themselves. Many letters from the frontlines were censored and many writers tended to understate the dreadful conditions on the front to avoid alarming family members. Other writers, however, exaggerated or even invented the events they describe. But letters do have an immediacy, an intimacy and a direct appeal for general readers, features that are often missing from other primary sources of information. At times, too, soldiers did use their letters as a means of expressing their true, innermost feelings that often had to be concealed from their fellow soldiers. Where this occurred the letters can be very revealing indeed. If used with care, letters from the battlefields can be a useful and valuable source of information. As with any primary source relating to an important historical event, letters from soldiers to their families should not be ignored. They have the potential to be sources of great historical value.

A feature of many of the letters of soldiers of 1914–18, one that continues to surprise people, is how literate the writers were. New Zealand is no exception here, as can be seen from the letters presented in this collection. Most New Zealand soldiers who served in the First World War wrote many letters home and wrote them very well. As a result of earlier education reforms in New Zealand a wider section of society than ever before were literate and they used every opportunity to communicate with loved ones back home.

The letters in this collection cover every major campaign in which New Zealanders fought during the war. It starts with a series of letters from the Gallipoli campaign. These feature a detailed account of the landing on 25 April 1915, as well as dealing with the offensive of August that year. While Gallipoli has cast a long shadow over the rest of New Zealand's involvement in the war, this is not the case here. Most of the letters in the collection deal with the New Zealanders on the Western Front and this reflects where New Zealand's main effort was made during the war. The battles of the Somme, Messines, Passchendaele and the advances of 1918 are all featured in the collection. Also presented are letters from the less well-known Sinai and Palestine campaign, where a brigade of New Zealand Mounted Rifles fought a long, mobile campaign from 1916–18 as part of an Anzac Mounted Division. One letter details the New Zealand Division's march into Germany in 1919 and the occupation of the German city of Cologne. This collection of letters covers an incredible sweep of territory and takes the reader from Gallipoli to the Rhineland of Germany.

Something that some may find unpalatable, but which is true nonetheless, is that throughout their experiences during the First World War, whether at Gallipoli, on the Western Front or in Sinai and Palestine, the New Zealanders earned a reputation as superb soldiers. Everywhere New Zealand soldiers fought in this war they acquitted themselves well. So much was this the case that one of the world's most well-known military historians, John Keegan, has written that in this war the New Zealanders' 'settler independence and skills with rifle and spade would win them a reputation as the best soldiers in the world during the twentieth century'.[11] While this is heady praise the cost of earning this enviable reputation should not be forgotten. The concluding section of this book highlights only part of the cost of New Zealand's involvement.

The First World War, a pivotal event in New Zealand's history, brought many changes to New Zealand. A leading Australian military historian has written that 'the influence of a major war is generally held to continue to shape a society for a century after its end'.[12] If this is so, and there is little reason to doubt it, New Zealand continues to live with the legacy of the First World War. In September 1917, just before the horrors of Passchendaele, a soldier penned the following memorable lines in his diary:

> Adieu, the years are a broken song,
> And the right grows weak in the strife with wrong,
> The lilies of love have a crimson stain,
> And the old days never will come again.[13]

The words neatly encapsulate the impact of the war on all the nations that took part. For New Zealand as much as any other country the 1914–18 war meant there were broken years ahead and the old days never did return.

Gallipoli

While the Gallipoli campaign was not the first action of the war for New Zealand soldiers — they had been involved in the capture of German Samoa and in the defence of the Suez Canal in February 1915 – it was certainly the most significant of these early encounters.

In terms of its origins, planning and execution the Gallipoli campaign remains one of the most controversial episodes in the history of the First World War. Initially it was meant to be a purely naval affair. The attempt to force open The Narrows as the gateway to Constantinople began on 19 February 1915. It immediately ran into problems. On 18 March a great armada of sixteen battleships, flotillas of cruisers and destroyers and hundreds of minesweepers set out to force The Narrows. Great things were expected of this combined British-French fleet, but when they failed to penetrate the Turkish minefields and lost six capital ships in one day the navy had to admit defeat. The navy proved incapable of dealing with the combination of the dense minefield laid across The Narrows and the Turkish artillery batteries on both sides of the straits. The only solution was to stage a landing to clear these shores.

The Mediterranean Expeditionary Force under General Sir Ian Hamilton was given this task and it was a formidable one. The Mediterranean Expeditionary Force consisted of the 29th, the Royal Naval, 1st Australian and Australian and New Zealand Divisions and the *Corps expeditionnaire d'Orient*, French troops of about division strength. The Turkish forces numbered six weak divisions of about 84,000, who had to guard about 150 miles of coastline. General Hamilton had nowhere near enough troops for the size of the task ahead. It was known at the time that the Australians and New Zealanders were only partially trained, were inexperienced and, it was felt, were of

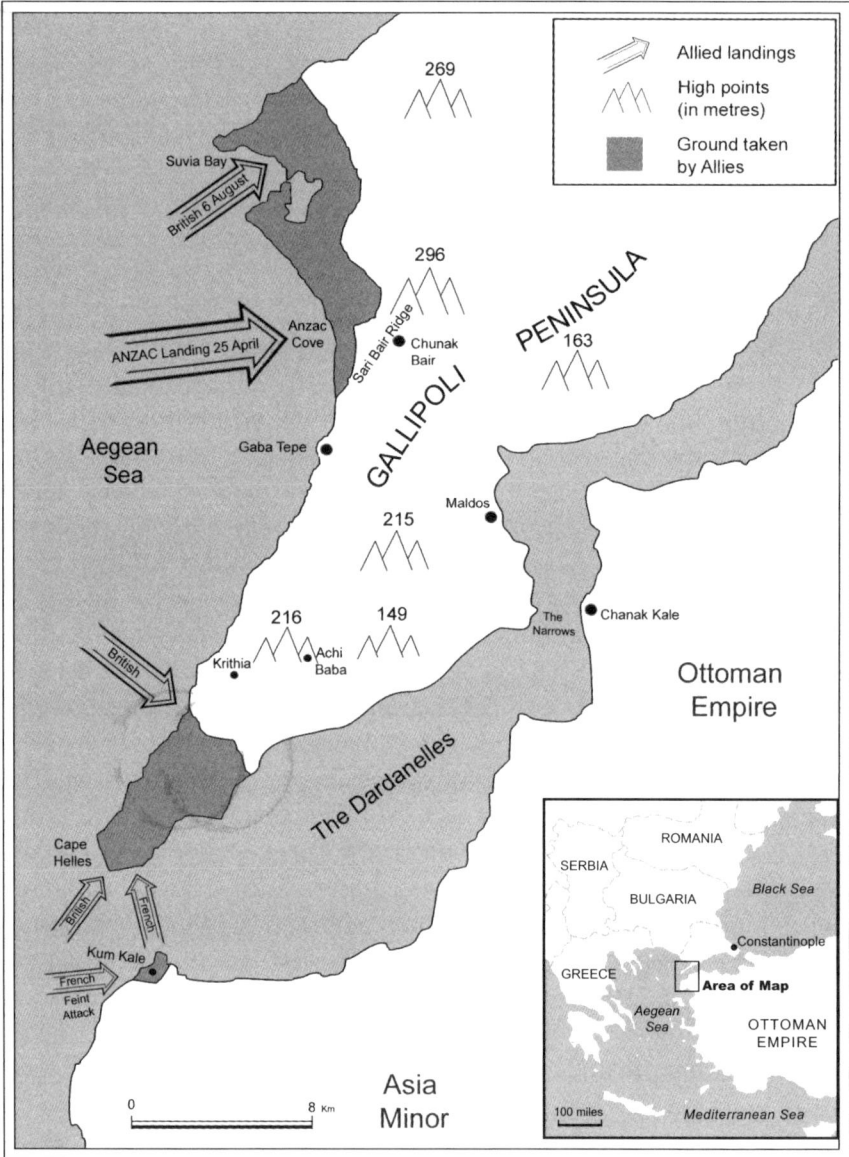

doubtful quality. As a result they were given a subordinate role in the initial landings, a sideshow within a sideshow. The Anzacs, as they were now designated, were to land to the north of Gaba Tepe while the British and French made the main assault at Cape Helles.

The Australians and New Zealanders landed on the Gallipoli Peninsula in the early hours of 25 April 1915. For reasons never satisfactorily explained, they landed a mile north of the gentle beach that had been selected as their landing area. On all three sides of what became Anzac Cove high cliffs dominated the area and overlooked the beach. The Australian and New Zealand soldiers who landed that morning knew they had to get as high and as deep as they could and tried to do so. Unfortunately, by late afternoon they had penetrated to a depth of a mile and a half, still one mile short of the summit of the dominating Sari Bair ridge. Owing to their exhaustion and the opposition of the Turkish defenders organised by Mustapha Kemal, they could get no further.

After the initial landing, the rest of the campaign involved trying to consolidate and expand the lodgement made on the first day. This peaked in the major offensive of August 1915 in which the Anzac forces played a lead part. It was during this attack that the New Zealanders captured and held for a short time the Chunuk Bair ridge, the furthest point inland that the Allied forces penetrated. By September though, with the failure of the August offensive, it was evident that the troops on Gallipoli were exhausted and should be evacuated. The troops were withdrawn three months later in what proved to be the most well-planned and well-executed operation of the whole campaign. It had lasted eight and a half months.

Gallipoli revealed the military potential and the natural talents of the New Zealand soldier, especially in his ability to adapt to difficult circumstances. Natural ability could not compensate for failures in planning, leadership, logistics and administration, however, and no soldiers in this war could afford to be committed to battle only half-trained. All of these failures contributed to the defeat on Gallipoli.

There are six letters in the Gallipoli section. Two of the letters de-scribe the landing of 25 April in considerable detail, 'a memorable day for Australia and New Zealand' as one of the letters so aptly com-ments. Both letters describe what it was like to be part of this significant event and they bring it alive for the reader. Four of the letters detail what life was like for the New Zealand soldiers throughout the long weeks of the Gallipoli campaign. This is important, because so much of the popular attention that has focused on the Gallipoli campaign remains riveted to the landing of 25 April. New Zealand soldiers spent many months on the Gallipoli peninsula. The dangers and hardships they endured — the flies and lice and the disease they spread, the dread-ful plight of the wounded, the harsh climate, the poor rations, the dangers from snipers and bombs — all of it features in the letters here. The last letter in this section indicates that even when the soldiers had left the peninsula they were still vulnerable to enemy action.

The losses on Gallipoli were staggering, but unfortunately this was only the first of many long casualty lists for New Zealand. The Turks, who neither buried nor counted their dead, lost approximately 300,000 men killed, wounded or missing. The Allies lost 265,000. One Allied division, the 29th, lost its strength twice over. New Zealand casualty rates are also extraordinary: 8566 New Zealanders served on the peninsula, 7473 were casualties. Of these, 2721 New Zealanders were killed in action or died from accidents and disease. Only 344 have known grave sites. Of the others, 252 were buried at sea, but the majority, some 1669, have no known grave, many lying where they fell in action.

As so many commentators have noted, New Zealand lost more than just many of its soldiers at Gallipoli. It also lost its innocence. While this is so, New Zealand at the same time discovered something about itself, as the first stirrings of a national identity emerged from the fighting on that far off peninsula in the Aegean Sea.

✄

Lieutenant Davies was wounded on Gallipoli but went on to serve in France where he won the Distinguished Service Order at Messines. He was wounded twice in France; the second wounding required the amputation of his leg. Robert Davies died in Palmerston North in May 1977. In this letter, he describes the landing at Anzac Cove (pictured).

Lemnos Harbour
Saturday 24 April

During the last week we have been making preparations to proceed to Dardanelles by practising disembarking, etc. Today we have been issued with maps and had the orders and plan of action explained. Every man has to carry three days' rations and 200 rounds of ammunition, as supplies will not be landed till sufficient ground is gained. During the afternoon all the cruisers and transports left the harbour in their turn to take up their positions. It was a great and grand sight to see transports leaving and cruisers and dreadnoughts sailing majestically past with bands playing and in their battle array. Great cheers were exchanged with the ships in harbour. In all there must be 80 transports and 40 man-of-war, exclusive of submarines, and hosts of torpedo destroyers and other small craft, such as minesweepers etc, so you can imagine the sight. We have a most important part to play in the attack. We land in a small bay north of Gaba Tepe point on the western side of the peninsula just directly opposite Maidos and work overland towards The Narrows and take the main road running down the centre, which completely cuts the Turks off in the south. We then command Maidos and The Narrows. The British and French land in the south and attack and join up with us later.

'Der Tag' (The Day)
Sunday 25 April

We rose at reveille on what was to be, as the evening proved, a memorable day for Australia and New Zealand. The weather was perfect, the sea like glass, surely in all our movements we have always been blessed with the most favourable circumstances. Ships going ahead of us had left their anchorages during the night and so had all the battleships. Our orders were to be at our landing point at 12 noon. This point is only six hours run from Lemnos. We left late, however, and arrived to disembark three hours late. Our New Zealand and Australian division was to commence the attack at 3.30 a.m., just as the British and French commenced theirs in the south, and some of our division left during the night, but as we are not required till later we were timed to leave this morning.

We were just clear of Lemnos Harbour when we heard the tremendous boom of guns just 30 miles off. This bombardment had started at 3.30 a.m. but had slackened off at 8 a.m. and continued again at 9 a.m. as we left. We held a church service on board amid the booming of the big guns.

At about midday we were just off the southwest end of the peninsula where the British and French were disembarking— the scene was wonderful! We passed quite close to them. Ten or twelve great battleships were covering their landing, amongst which was the *Queen Elizabeth*, sending forth her huge shells. The fire was wonderful — every shot told. The bombardment was a wonderful sight, at each shot from the guns huge heaps of earth shot into the air and Turks also, where the shells struck trenches — all this could be seen distinctly. The land was fairly level country and landing was fairly easy as far as we could judge. We passed them for two hours, and the roar of the cannon was thunderous, and the scream of the shells very weird, our fire did not seem to be answered very much from the shore. A little further up the coast we could see our own landing point and our ships inshore discharging. We were supposed to be in the third relay, but we lost our place as we were late. As we drew near we could hear a great battle going on and we knew our landing was being stubbornly resisted. Rifle fire rang out from both sides and machine guns fired continuously. Our landing was covered by HMS *Queen*, *Prince of Wales*, *Majestic*, *Triumph*, *London* and the destroyers *Bulldog*, *Chelmar* and another. The cruisers were pelting the hell into the Turks as we came up.

Our landing place is a small bay on the west coast of the peninsula just above The Narrows. The beach is good, but the hills rise immediately from the beach to a height in the highest point on our left of about 600 feet. Steep gullies and ravines are in the face of these hills and they are covered with a thick low scrub.

Our landing started at about 3.30 a.m. when the warships landed some of the Australians. Barbed wire entanglements were found in the water at one place, but these were avoided. The Australians were just getting ashore when a murderous fire was opened on them and shrapnel fell round the boats and killed some before they could land. In the face of this, however, they landed and succeeded in driving the Turks from the two front trenches — with the bayonet — to the top of the ridge . . .

The casualties on our side were heavy, but that can only be expected under the circumstances — landing against such odds and immediate rising country was a great credit to New Zealanders and Australians as the warships could only cover them by pounding away, they could not locate every battery they had as they were so wonderfully concealed.

By midday, when the Turks were driven back, we took the ridge and four Krupp guns and some machine guns. A great number of our men were injured by falls while scaling the hillside and gullies. When the Turks were driven back the Australians chased them, but sufficient troops were not yet landed to go so far on. Consequently they had to drop back a little in the afternoon. However, they had cleared the face of the hill for a good distance. Snipers were all over the hillside and picked off the officers galore, many being shot dead and some seriously wounded. Then we ourselves came up to our anchorage at 3.30 p.m. and began to disembark. Our men had been watching this bombardment all day coming up the coast, and when we came to our own position all were ready and steady and eager to get ashore. Really, one would have thought they were going for a trip across Wellington Harbour the way they went off, instead of forcing a landing amid shrapnel and bullets and the thunderous roar, rattle and vibrating of the big guns.

The behaviour of the men was wonderful, all cheery and bright as could be.

The destroyers were used for landing the troops, with the assistance of boats and barges. Our destroyer, *Bulldog*, came alongside at about 5 p.m. and took off 500 men just as there was a great lull in the fighting and one man was heard to call out: 'By Jove, they must have a union here, they have knocked off at five p.m.' Well, it was lucky that our boys got ashore during the lull, as very little shrapnel struck them and all landed safe. Before the second load went off from our ship a big load of wounded in two big barges came alongside and we had to start taking them in, as the hospital ship was full . . .

I thought the sight of wounded might unnerve them but it had no effect. The second load left at about 8.30 p.m. and all landed safely in the dark. Rain then commenced to fall.

I am left aboard with a party in charge of the stores and wagons etc. in the hold, which I have to unload first before I can get ashore.

As the second lot moved away Royden McDowell, my great

friend, called from the darkness an Egyptian farewell. Great crowds of wounded came aboard and the sights were awful. I was up all night with the few men I had left with me, taking wounded men aboard and attending to them. Medical aid was procured from HMS *Queen*. The sights were terrible and I do not know how I stood it all. I only pray I have seen as bad as I will see. Such butchery one would not think possible. We now have 500 wounded aboard, mostly all Australians, some already dead and many dying.

Some New Zealanders are amongst the first wounded, which shows that those who were first ashore were somewhat cut up. The New Zealanders did splendidly when once they disembarked. As one wounded Australian said to me, 'I thought our fellows could fight, but by — those New Zealanders, when they came up they gave them hell!' Today's casualties are estimated at over 4000.

All the wounded consider that the Germans are behind the guns. They say the Turks cannot shoot but the snipers hidden in the scrub are good, and a great annoyance. Officers were picked off on the beach by snipers only a few hundred yards away and the shrapnel also has claimed many officers before they have really landed.

Monday 26 April

Heavy bombardment and fighting started again at daybreak. Our balloon and seaplanes reconnoitred at daylight and then a most terrific bombardment followed from our ships. It was found that the Turks were reinforcing and strengthening on our left. Tons of earth flew into the air from the Turks' trenches on the top and face of the big hill on our left and our men could be seen creeping up steadily, pouring murderous fire on to the enemy. The Turks evacuated their position about midday, when our chaps gained the main top ridge on our right, and the artillery — now ashore — was seen being dragged by men to the top of a low ridge on our right flank and four guns were got going and went like mad all day doing great work. Our infantry scurried up the hillface and could be seen entrenching. More troops are now ashore and our right wing with the howitzers seems to be well established.

The thunder and screaming of the guns cannot be imagined. The *Queen Elizabeth* and other ships came up to us today and knocked things about over the other side of the hill where the Turks are reinforcing and also on the topmost high hill on our left where Turkish well-concealed batteries still worry us. The *Queen Elizabeth* just about shifts the whole hill when she starts. I am awfully anxious to get ashore to give a hand, but we cannot discharge until we have taken sufficient ground to enable us to land stores. We are anchored quite close in so I am forced to be an eyewitness.

Casualties are not so numerous today, although a great many wounded have come aboard.

Tonight the Turks are shelling our batteries, now established on our right, and it looks as though our chaps must be getting it bad.

Shrapnel is falling like rain all down our face of the hill and on to the beach where our reserves are dug in.

Our ships are replying at intervals and are paying attention to the high hill on our extreme left where the Turks have some batteries which are annoying us and threatening our left and which are hard to locate.

Several shells have been fired at the transports, but all have fallen round us into the water and no notice has been taken of them, being only shrapnel.

⚬

Letter of Lieutenant Fred McKee of the 2ⁿᵈ Canterbury Battalion (pictured). Two letters dealing with Lieutenant McKee's death on the Somme in September 1916 appear on pages 63–65. This long letter, written from diary extracts, has been abridged in places.

New Zealand Base, Alexandria

I have long put off writing the full account of our doings since leaving Zeitoun for our big fight in the Dardanelles. But here goes, without any preliminary remarks.

We left our old camp at Zeitoun at about 4 o'clock on the afternoon of April 4th and marched to Palais de Koubeh Station about 2 and a half miles with full pack up. Entraining a few hours later we arrived at Alexandria at 5 a.m. next morning. On the wharf we were struck by the picturesque look of the Zouaves, of whom there were a large number of machine-gunners awaiting embarkation. They showed us the simple mechanism of their guns, of which they had cause to be proud. We embarked on the *Itonus* at 8 a.m. and discovered she had been fitted out as a troopship for some months, having taken a load of Indian troops to England, a load of Australians to Egypt and then she was to take 12th and 13th Companys of Canterbury Battalion, 2 Company of the Wellington Battalion and a detachment of the Army Service Corps to the Dardanelles. Lieutenant Colonel Malone was the CO of the ship. We left the wharf at 3.45 a.m. on the 11th and anchored in the stream for an hour while a steam launch and two barges were secured with a stout wire rope for towing . . .

Sunday 25 April. A perfect morning. Weighed anchor at 6.15 a.m. and moved out. We expected to land under fire and be in action by 1 p.m.

1 p.m. Our ship is supposed to do 9 or 10 knots, but she seems slower by far, for we have a good way to go yet. One unending roar of guns is quite distinct now and fairly shakes the ship. The day is very warm and the sea quite calm. I have raisins and still another ration issued to us, making a total of three for each man to carry. Posted up outside the ship's Orderly Room we read this morning:

Force Order
(Special)
General Headquarters
21 April 1915

Soliders of France and of the King!
Before us lies an adventure unprecedented in modern war. Together with our comrades of the fleet, we are about to force a landing upon an open beach, in face of positions which have been vaunted by our enemies as impregnable.

The landing will be made good by the help of God and the Navy; the positions will be stormed, and this war brought one step nearer to a glorious close.

'Remember,' said Lord Kitchener, when bidding adieu to your commander, 'remember, once you set foot on the Gallipoli Peninsula you must fight the thing through to a finish.'

The whole world is watching our progress. Let us prove worthy of the great feat of arms entrusted to us.

Ian Hamilton
General

So we knew what was to come and as we steamed up the coast the booming of the guns came across the sea louder and louder as we got nearer. At 2 p.m. we could see quite clearly the battleships firing away at the forts at Cape Helles and trenches and great heaps of earth flung high in the air. First you could see the vivid flashes and dense clouds of smoke, sometimes enveloping the ships from view for a few minutes, then came the reports of the guns, a few seconds later more flashes and the smoke of the shells bursting.

I am sure those Tommies had a hard time of it that day and all the time there was a terrific bombardment going on. At 3.45 we were off Gaba Tepe with the rest of the transports that had brought the Australasians and at last dropped anchor. We could then hear the rattle of machine guns and rifles. Some of the troops off other ships had landed and were then hard at it. We got onto a destroyer and the remainder into a large barge and made for the shore at a good speed, stopping within half a mile or so of the shore.

While waiting there several boatloads of wounded passed us whom, of course, we cheered lustily, not that they needed it much, for they were cheerful enough. Stray bullets went 'flop' when they struck the water within a few feet of us and every few minutes four or five shrapnel shells would burst overhead, but they could not get our range, for we kept dodging a bit. And while we waited for our turn in the cutters we just smoked and talked. Eventually our Company (12th) were all ashore by 7 p.m. Forming up on the beach, we got tools (picks and shovels) and a few cases of ammunition and off we went, guided by a Staff Officer, for the extreme left of the whole position, from the sea upwards for a few hundred yards.

I was sent out in front with a few men as covering party while our Company dug in, for at that time our left flank seemed unprotected. I expect the warships were watching it that day, but it was necessary to entrench there at night. Well, we went out and had to keep low, of course, so as to catch the first glimpse if the enemy appeared.

It was drizzling slightly and a cold wind blowing made it bitterly cold notwithstanding our thick overcoats and oil sheets (of course, we had no blankets). It took all night to dig in and we were not sorry when the sun shone again and we were able to get some breakfast.

Monday 26 April. Along the beach at intervals were three boats with dead Australians sitting and lying in different attitudes. Poor fellows! They had done their duty at all events, even if they did not set foot on the shore and I'm sure they have been avenged doubly. Ah! But it made a man's blood boil that sight on the first morning.

The bombardment of the warships and the crackling of machine guns and rifles continued all day, the noise from the big guns sounded deafening, situated as we were under steep hills.

The landing place was very like Tasman Bluffs in parts, straight up and down in others, with steep scrub-covered spurs, and in places twice or three times the height. At 11 a.m. we moved up the same spur a little higher and entrenched again. That spur was like climbing the side of a house with full pack up, too. This spur was then our left flank and up it ran the wires (telephone) from headquarters up to the firing line on what is termed 'Walkers Ridge'.

It was very quiet where we were and all day (and night too) men sweated and toiled up this steep spur carrying water in kerosene tins and provisions from the stores on the beach and often helped their wounded comrades on their way to the dressing station.

But what won our admiration was the cool daring and tireless energy of the Red Cross men and stretcher-bearers. It was a sight never to be forgotten to see that endless stream of wounded being carried on stretchers, some hobbling with a mate's assistance and others striding down by themselves. I saw several go down like this with a bullet through the back, the work of some hiding sniper behind our lines.

Tuesday 27th. Fighting recommenced at dawn and at 12 noon was very heavy. The Turks were replying with shrapnel to our naval guns, which made a deafening roar and the earth shake under our feet, but it's grand to hear them all the same (when they are your own) and it gave us a feeling of security at that time. The enemy were repulsed, but their guns were hard to locate for they had such a number of places to conceal them.

We set sentries and turned in, but pulled out again at 11 p.m. to move a little higher up the spur. Such are the little annoyances we get in the army, but you have to get used to it.

Wednesday 28 April. Fighting continued, but more in sharp, short bursts to rapid fire . . . The Turks kept on blazing day and night for the first week or so. Fewer wounded came down today, so our fellows up on Walkers Ridge must be properly dug in by now. But the enemy have beastly troublesome snipers, who are crack shots and who keep sniping our boys from the most unexpected places. And some of the beggars made themselves look like a rhododendron bush. With face painted it was very difficult to pick him up, but once he was 'spotted' it was 'Goodbye sniper' for one rifle was not trusted to pot him.

The enemy's artillery was less active today, and so far they are using shrapnel, and occasionally some small ordinary shells are dropped quite harmlessly out in the sea. At 11 a.m. we moved lower down the spur and spent the afternoon making dugouts for ourselves (and others after us) behind the firing line on the inside slope. It was a good place and quite safe from shrapnel and strays.

Thursday 29 April. Had a good sleep in our 'bivvys' last night. The first since landing. We had a spell today, including a swim in the sea, a shave and a wash. I'd almost forgotten how to do it. You'd be surprised how soon you get used to having no wash when you get up. But water was scarce even for drinking, a water bottle a day, and being fairly warm weather, by the time you had made two cups of tea and quenched your thirst during the heat of the day, there wasn't enough to even clean your teeth with, let alone such luxuries as washing your face and hands. Less naval and field artillery firing today and we are all getting used to trench life and the whistling of shells and bullets over our heads. There was plenty of tucker today, too, so we had rather a happy day of it. It was reported today that there were several of the enemy captured in our lines wearing Australian and New Zealand uniforms.

Friday 30 April. We spent the morning road-making up the spur, behind the firing line a few yards, from 6–10 a.m. Another platoon then relieved us and we were not sorry, for we had grafted hard, the road being badly needed to get some artillery up into position. Have now been here five days and have not seen a Turk or fired a shot yet, however somebody had to do the work that we were on so we did not growl. But all the same we should have liked to have got into the trenches on top where they were having all the shooting.

In the evening our Company was sent out about a half mile in advance of the left flank and took up three positions on the tops of spurs.

Here we dug in all night as the ground was very hard and full of scrub roots . . .

Monday 3 May. We had a real good sleep last night and we deserved it. Had also a good rest in the trenches and saw a transport hit by a Turkish shell; at first we thought it was all up, but she just hauled her anchor up and steamed quietly away. At 7 p.m. occurred the heaviest bombardment we had heard; also a terrible rattle of rifles and machine guns. We heard the firing line gained 800 yards . . .

Thursday 6 May. Last night at 11 p.m. all the New Zealand Infantry Brigade embarked in punts and then on to destroyers, our Company being mostly on the destroyer *Mosquito*. After an hour's run we disembarked . . . ashore at Cape Helles, where we slept on the beach until morning. Then we marched inland a couple of miles and made more dugouts in the reserve lines. The 2nd Australian Infantry Brigade, with our Brigade, had been sent down to reinforce the British Regulars, who had been sadly decimated in the landing and subsequent fighting.

From here we went and watched several batteries of French 75s. They are wonderful guns: so simple and so quickly loaded, but they play havoc with the Turks. We also watched the British 18-pounders and a couple of big 60-pounders. The French infantry, covered by their artillery, gained a considerable distance — approximately 3000 yards, I believe. The Turks were unable to locate our batteries, but sent a few shells within 100 yards or so of us. But we are beginning to get used to it now.

Occasionally they put some shrapnel over us, but their shooting is pretty poor.

Friday 7 May. We got a full marching order at 2 p.m. and moved over to our left and in advance of our dugouts, where we slept in old trenches. We were shelled for a while at dusk with shrapnel and common shell, but there were very few casualties (Colonel Peerless was hit here, I heard later).

Saturday 8 May. We advanced in artillery formation under fire across some open ground and then up a nullah (a creek with steep banks) for some distance. From here we suddenly doubled across the open ground behind the Worcester's trenches and flopped down as quickly as possible for the bullets were playing all round. After lying

here a few minutes we advanced to the firing line (in parties) which was
about 100 or 150 yards in front and held by the Munster Fusiliers, and
weren't they pleased to see reinforcements, too. At 5.30 p.m. there was a
general advance along the whole line covered by French and British
field artillery and warships. Off we went and by Jove, it fairly rained
bullets, machine guns and rifles were let loose by the Turks!

But we only got about 300 yards and then made head cover till
dark and our losses were very heavy. Poor Lieutenant Forsyth was killed
in the advance with a bullet through the head. We were all very sorry to
lose our Platoon Commander, as he was a good officer and popular.

It was a brilliant charge that, but it cost us a lot of casualties: more
than the landing did and still we were a long way from Krithia. It was
here I got three bullets through my clothing and equipment, and in my
section C.C. Gibbs was killed. G.H. White died of wounds a few days
later, and also wounded were F. Bruning, D.R. McLeod and C. Parsons.

After dark we entrenched as hard as we could go until about 3
a.m., when I received a two gallon jar of rum and issued it out to 128
men and I awakened some of the poor beggars who had fallen asleep, so
tired were they, but there was not one growl when they knew what I had.

I was told a good many times that morning that 'I had saved a
man's life' to which I usually replied, 'All right, hurry up and get that
rum down. I don't want to stand up here all night behind the trench for
the Turks' amusement.'

We were all mixed up, Australians, Wellington, Auckland, Otago
and Canterbury, but that is always the way after a charge. Two or three
times in the night the enemy opened fire and we could see long lines of
rifle flashes, and then both the Turks and ourselves threw up flares and
you could see almost as plain as day.

Sunday 9 May. There were numbers of dead Turks lying about
quite near us and the stench was awful, and the Turks kept putting
bullets through these swelled-up gentlemen and you can guess how it
was eating your meals within a few feet of them. It was pretty quiet
today, except the snipers were having a 'fly' at each other. We then
deepened our trenches to about four feet when we had to stop, owing to
water, so then we built up the parapet and after that had a sleep in the
bottom of the trench. In the evening I went down to the 'nullah' and
made some tea . . .

Thursday 13 May. We left the trenches last night at 10 p.m. having
been relieved by the East Lancashire Territorials. What a tramp that

was down to the old dugouts in a drenching rain with stray bullets whizzing close by at times!

We just got back there the best way we could and most of us slept out anywhere in the rain, covered with our oilsheets. But we woke up pretty wet and miserable in the morning and parties straggled in from all directions, dead tired, and our dugouts were half full of water, but afterwards it cleared up so we bailed the water out and cut up biscuit tins to make a floor with. A muster parade was held at 11 a.m. to account for all casualties . . .

Thursday 20 May. We woke up to find ourselves off the old position at Anzac. We went ashore in punts towed by pinnaces and two men were killed by snipers on the way in.

Friday 21 May. Last night at 6.30 p.m. an attack developed and as we were in support that night we moved to our position and remained on the look out. We were not needed, however, so returned to the dugouts in 'Rest Gully' this morning. We learned when we returned that the New Zealand Mounteds, Australian Light Horse and remaining three infantry brigades had had a good deal of fun repulsing a big Turkish attack, causing them several thousands of casualties and with very few to our fellows. Our Mounteds had arrived at Anzac the day after we sailed for Cape Helles.

There was an artillery duel for a while, and occasionally heavy bursts of rifle fire. I was on fatigue this morning with the party trench-digging . . .

Sunday 23 May. Last evening there was a great commotion at sea — destroyers darted about in all directions as a hostile submarine had been sighted. The usual firing occurred last night; also I slept in a blanket for the first time since leaving the *Itonis*. It's a quiet, warm day so instead of going down to church I stayed 'at home' and wrote to all of you at home which, from letters I have received, was the first you received from me on the Peninsula. That seems funny, for I wrote twice before that. I've resorted to pencil because the pen would not work, but I know you won't mind.

This morning I went for a swim down on the beach, which is only a few hundred yards from where we are. We are now getting three or four packets of cigarettes and two issues of rum a week.

I'm not a lover of spirits, but that rum is very welcome at times and is a great pick-me-up. You see even teetotallers have a 'nip' sometimes and I don't blame them for it's better than medicine in some ways.

Monday 24 May. Our first armistice (and last I think) was held from 7.30 a.m. till 4 p.m. today and it seemed quite strange to have quietness again for so long.

From our battalion a large number of men were sent up to carry in wounded (if any) and to bury the dead. I have often since regretted not joining up myself and having a look, but you can't imagine what it would look like, to see, as it was in one place, 8 acres covered in Turkish dead, and in many places bodies lying three or four deep across each other. The majority of these were the result of the Turks' attack a few nights previous and those who went up said they had been there quite long enough to be unpleasant to handle. You can't imagine what dead Turks smell like, but you will perhaps when I liken it to sulphuretted hydrogen. If you've never tried that, ask a chemist to let you.

Tuesday 25 May. Our battalion was on outlying picquet last night and it was rainy and lightning and thundering a treat and we were a bit sorry looking this morning when we came off. We could not sleep, so just sat listening to the rifles and bombs. A party of us were on road-making for three hours this morning and after coming off witnessed from some distance the sinking of the *Triumph*. It was an awful sight to see a warship go down. That set the torpedo destroyers going again, and the transports were then withdrawn to a place of greater safety . . .

Saturday 29 May. Our battalion was the inlying picquet again last night. There was heavy artillery fire, also rifles, machine guns and bombs. The enemy blew up a portion of our trench at Quin's Post and occupied it, but were soon driven out of it again — considerable firing continued all day . . .

Wednesday 2 June. 12 and 13 Companys were moved up into the firing line at 11 a.m., all our Company joining in except a few men required on various fatigues, such as carrying water and cooked food and tea to those in the trenches. Our platoon is occupying No 4 Post, which the Turks blew up the other night. Here the trenches are, I suppose, between 15 and 20 yards apart, and all day and night in shifts our miners and engineers are toiling away, mining the Turks occasionally, but chiefly to countermine or prevent the Turks blowing us up again. In parts we had places within 3 or 4 yards of the Turks, from which we threw bombs into the Turks' trenches, but they seemed to have plenty of these and they let us know it. The weather is getting very hot and the air is not too pure either. However, disinfectant makes it a *wee bit* more pleasant . . .

Saturday 5 June. We went back to the firing line at midday. A party from Canterbury Battalion and Auckland attacked on the night of the 5th and for a while 'twas like 'Hell let loose'. They took the trench easily enough, but they were ordered to retire at 6 a.m., for the Turks made it too hot with bombs and enfilade fire. Out of the 25 who advanced from our company, 17 were casualties. Lieutenant Roul and Sergeant Guy were both wounded and Captain Griffiths told me I was to be acting platoon commander.

Poor Captain Goulding was killed at about 7 a.m. of the 6th June. He was a great favourite in our Company.

Monday 7 June. We were relieved at midday and as we had had no sleep the previous two nights we were very tired, but the flies were an awful pest and made it almost impossible to sleep in the daytime.

Tuesday 8 June. We returned again to the trenches at noon and were relieved again at 8 a.m. on June 9th by the Wellington Battalion, then we went a half mile or so down 'Shrapnel Gully' to have eight days out of the firing line. Thus ended my first experience of 'rather warm' defensive fighting, for Quin's was an important post and had to be held at any cost. Well, it was rather a nerve-racking job that first week, with bombs alighting near one without giving any warning and expecting to be sky high any moment. But we didn't worry too much after a while, for we thought, 'If we are to go up, we'll go up and let's hope we'll land in a soft place when we come down.' That's how nine men out of every ten take it now; if a man is to stop a bullet or an 8-inch shell or a few shrapnel he'll just stop them and *nothing* can alter that!

This new gully was termed 'Canterbury Gully' and here we made our homes for a week, in the form of dugouts. I can now tell you heaps about Turkish subsoil, but perhaps I had better not weary you with the different classes. But I've seen some lovely slopes for apple growing and I'm sure the subsoil must be all right. I'll have to go and try it with my 'toothpick' some day . . .

Friday 18 June. 12th and 13th Companys breakfasted early and left 'Canterbury Gully' for another spell in the trenches at 8 a.m. We found it much quieter this time, for our bomb-throwers, having now more bombs at their disposal, could now throw back two every time the Turks threw one, consequently they were getting a bit 'jollied' and fewer came over into our trenches. There was a slight artillery duel at times, but it was a lot quieter than last time. Lieutenant Gallaway from Otago is now our new platoon commander, he came with the 4th reinforcements.

Saturday 19 June. 12th and 13th Companys were relieved by 1st and 2nd Companys. There was the usual routine in the trenches — sniping with rifles and periscopic rifles, which enable us to snipe away without exposing ourselves above the parapet. We are now occupying well-constructed, deep trenches, and the miners have now made us pretty safe against the mines of the enemy. We are to continue for 24 hours in the trenches and 24 hours out in the rest gully, until the 25th, when we are to move down to 'Canterbury Gully' again.

Sunday 20 June. We went into the trenches again this morning and were jolly pleased to receive our mail and read letters in the trenches. I received one each from Dad and Mabel both dated May 5th. It's getting very warm here now and the air is not at all pleasant and the flies buzz round by the million — you can't imagine how thick — they make our meals rather unpleasant. Our bomb throwers continue to do good work . . .

Thursday 24 June. We went into the trenches again at 9 a.m. for our last 24 hours. It's very quiet indeed now, for we have now gained superiority of fire and the bomb throwers give them more than they wanted. I could not stick it so Lieutenant Galloway sent me down to the doctor at 9 p.m. and I slept below till the morning . . .

Saturday-Sunday-Monday 26–27–28 June. I have been feeling pretty seedy. Ate little. On the morning of 28th at 9 a.m. I was sent to the beach by Colonel Peerless, who had then returned from hospital. From the jetty a boatload of us were towed out to the hospital ship where the stretcher cases were hoisted aboard and the remainder of us were taken over to the fleet sweeper HMS *Clacton*, which weighed anchor at about 12 noon. Passing Ache Baba we could see the shells of our artillery bursting ahead of our advancing infantry. There were about 200 of us aboard altogether. We reached a 'Tommy' hospital at 7 p.m. that evening. There is no use wearying you of how I spent the next few days.

On July 5th I thought I was fit to go back, so was discharged. I got aboard HMS *Clacton* again at 5 p.m. after being some hours on head-quarters ship *Aragon*. We weighed anchor at about 7.30 p.m. and arrived back at Anzac Cove at 1 a.m. and I then made my way back to the Company, which came out of the trenches at Quin's Post at 9 a.m. on the 6th. I wrote home. I soon discovered I had been a fool for leaving Lemnos before I was properly well again.

Wednesday 7 July. Our company was in trenches again. I had to report to the doctor again and being excused duty remained below. I was very weak in the legs — had no appetite . . .

Thursday-Friday-Saturday 15–16–17 July. We get better treatment here and good food, but I ate very little. Doctor put me on two baby bottles of stout a day and I disposed of them all right. We have a perfect view of the harbour and shipping and at one time there were four hospital ships, which looked well at night with their long rows of green lights and the red crosses in the centre. I read a good deal at times, but could not sleep much and to make it worse fleas etc. were rather numerous . . .

Monday 19 July. Doctor told me I should have to go to Egypt, so after a lot of hanging about we got aboard the hospital ship *London* lying in stream.

Tuesday 20 July. Had quite an uneventful trip to Alexandria where we arrived at about 5 p.m. on July 22nd.

Egypt once more after all. I wondered when leaving whether I should ever see Egypt again. But here we are safe, even if not sound.

From the docks men were sent in all directions in the train or motor cars to various hospitals. I was, as you know, sent to the 17th General at Victoria College so I think I have almost finished my account since you have heard by letters of my doings since.

And now I hope this account is not too long for you to read. I may have left out parts and I may have put in unnecessary stuff, but I suppose the censor will decide that. However, I hope he does not cross out too much.

Yours affectionately

Fred

⚔

Victor Christophers (pictured). There are two letters written by Victor; the third letter describes his fate on Gallipoli. Victor Christophers was one of four brothers who served in the First World War. All four were killed.

4 May 1915

My dear Mother, Father

I wrote you a few lines yesterday; I think this will reach you by a later mail. You will no doubt read full accounts of the landing at the Dardanelles in the newspapers, but I will tell you all I have heard about it. I cannot vouch for the accuracy of what I write, but they are just tales told by the wounded who have returned. After waiting about in the transports for two or three weeks, our fellows made a landing on Sunday the 25th April. The Allies landed on six different beaches. The Australians and New Zealanders landed at a place called Sari Bair. Steep slopes arise from this beach and scrub about 2 feet high covers the slopes. All seemed quiet until the landing parties neared the shore, but when they got within a few chains of the beach, concealed batteries, machine guns and riflemen opened a deadly fire. Things were very thick. Some boats were sunk before they reached the beach and to add to the difficulty of landing barbed-wire entanglements were found under the water. Casualties were heavy. Some Australian companies were nearly wiped out, but boatloads rushed ashore and the colonials scrambled up the slopes and went for the Turks with their bayonets. Excitement was intense. I believe seven stokers who were watching the fight from one transport jumped overboard, picked up bayonets and joined in the mêlée. Some of the boat crews also left their boats on the beach and joined in the fun. The warships opened fire. The *Queen Elizabeth* or *Lizzie* as the fellows call her, the largest, latest warship in the navy, did especially good work. Her shots are deafening and are deadly effective. The Turkish batteries are concealed in the scrub and it was difficult to pick them up. Landing parties located these and signalled the range to the warships. One shot from the *Queen Elizabeth* would settle anything. Some Turkish warships attempted to join in the fight, but whenever they caught sight of *Lizzie* they immediately made themselves scarce.

The Turks would not stand up to the bayonet and all who could run, fled as soon as the colonials reached the trenches. The Turks did a lot of damage with sharpshooters, who were hidden in the scrub. Many wore khaki similar to our uniforms and it was often difficult to pick enemies from friends. The Turks are mostly led by German officers.

In the meantime, landings had been made on the other beaches by English troops, while French troops landed on the Asiatic side. The

Allies have now secured a strong position on the Gallipoli Peninsula and we are waiting to hear of further developments.

Some of our men were too eager and chased the enemy too far and came right up against the enemy's gun and were forced to retire with heavy losses. The Otago Southland men suffered least of all. Their officer commanding, Colonel Moore, entrenched his men as soon as he got them in a good position and this is what the others should have done.

Amongst the wounded who have arrived here is Alds Grant, of the Star Football Club. Many of the New Zealand wounded went to Malta. Every day ships are arriving here with wounded. Fellows treat a wound through the arm or leg very lightly. It is surprising how quickly a wound heals. Many who returned here last week wounded are on their way back to the front.

The navy are very enthusiastic over the achievements of the army and the soldiers' chief amusement is to watch the warships bombarding.

Hope Censure pass this.

Love from

Victor

Sunday 23 May 1915

My dear Mother, Father

I sent you a postcard in the last mail. I did not have time to write. We have been kept pretty busy lately. I am writing this during a halt on the way to a new position. It is a lovely summer's morning, 8.30 a.m. I would still be in bed if I were at home. We were up at 4.30 this morning. We are just beside the sea and are camped in a picturesque spot, reminding me of Stewart Island. I cannot keep comparing the beauty of our surroundings, the lovely sunsets, the calmness of the sea, with the death-struggle we are engaged in. If mother were here she might say with a good deal of justification, 'Where every prospect pleases and only man is vile.' The life is sometimes strenuous; you get weary with continual work, want to sleep, but when we get a spell, life is very pleasant here. It is just like a picnic. We get a swim in the sea nearly every day, you soon get used to the shells. 'A miss is as good as a mile' at this game — you soon get cunning about the shells. You learn to know when they are coming your way by the burst and by the singing sound you hear. When they sound close, you dive for the nearest cover. You do not feel half as nervous as you would suspect when going under fire for the first time. The Turks were dropping a few odd sheets of shrapnel when we were landing. I had the same sort of feeling I often have had when going to a dentist. But, as when going continually to a dentist, you get used to it and learn not to cry out before you are hurt.

But we are having a rosy time compared with those who landed first. They had a very hard time of it. The account I wrote while at Alexandria of the landing of the colonials is fairly correct. I am forbidden to say more about it now. You will understand I cannot write anything with regard to our operations. I have seen the places our fellows stormed — mostly all landslips — and the taking of that is equal to any feat I have ever read of in British warfare.

I had not been ashore two minutes when I met Archie Macdonald. It was a stroke of luck. I may not see him again for several weeks. Val Stocker was camped a few yards from us. Both are quite well and sound. I met George Tothill last night. He was wounded in the leg, but is quite well again now. It is remarkable how few wounds are serious. You need not worry if I am ever posted as wounded. Very few die from wounds. George told me Charlie Hudson was all right and has been promoted to lance corporal. By the way, I have just heard that I am supposed to have been shot. Some of our fellows arrived a few days ago and I met some of them this morning. Eric Davidson from the Bluff has just been congratulating me on being alive. Of course, it is just another rumour. We are always hearing of the death of someone and meeting them a few days after. None of our section have been hurt yet. We are camped in a very healthy spot and there is very little sickness. I am very well. This is much healthier than Cairo.

You might let Aunt Sara and any others who should ask, know that I am quite well and that I will be able to write very few letters. I have a very small stock of stationery and I must keep all I have to write to you. Whenever you write will you please enclose a few envelopes and sheets of notepaper. Never make a parcel of them, because parcels so often mis-carry. There are no shops this way and I must not carry more than is absolutely necessary.

We are very well fed here, better than we've been since leaving New Zealand. We get supplied with tobacco and matches and get rum served out twice a week. We don't think much of the prohibitionists who want to stop our rum and beer. It is the one luxury we have. I have never met a prohibitionist in the army.

Dear Mrs Christophers

I had letters from Ernest today. This is what he said about Victor: 'Poor dear old Vic, how we all miss him, I can't say what a loss he is to me, he was the only fellow in the section I could speak to freely. Now his body lies at the foot of our little hill, with another of our small gun team beside him. Vic and I never did agree upon souls, but if there is a place for them I guess he's near the top of the class with a place in the sun. The waves break along the bay a little way from his feet. The sun climbs over a clear sky above the tree that shades him and sets in front of his biscuit box cross every golden evening and birds fly over and flowers bloom and old Vic takes no notice. But also the rifles crack and the big guns roar and the bombs thud and he takes as little heed of that, so maybe he's as well off.'

I hope, Mrs Christophers, that you had some word yourself by the same mail. Even if you did, I expect this will interest you.

Very sincerely yours

Faith Royds

James ('Will') Harvey (pictured) died of wounds received at Gallipoli on 2 September 1915. He was buried at sea on the way to Malta.

Anzac Trenches
26 July 1915

My Dear Mother
  I think it's up to me to send a few lines along; letter writing is
quite a job here owing to a scarcity of material and censorship. Well,
here goes; we left camp about 8.30 p.m. on 8th May, marched about 2
miles to the station with our full packs up, arrived at the station about
10 p.m., filed into the carriages and were away by 12.30 p.m., Alexandria
6.30 a.m.; marched straight on to the transport; about 9 o'clock we were
allowed on the wharf and had several nice cups of tea, provided by the
YWCA. The four of us then hired a cab and went to see the sights.
  We have been inoculated twice for cholera.
  The European quarter of Alexandria is lovely.
  The same evening we sailed for our destination.
  The transport was a fine ship and the voyage was uneventful. We
landed after dark on the islands of the Grecian Archipelago, which
were beautiful. We landed on the 12th and could hear the rifles crack-
ing on the ridges above the landing. Most of us thought we would be
into it straight away. The means of coming ashore were arranged this
way: from transport to destroyer, to lighters, to a small jetty and ashore.
After sorting things up a wee bit, they marched us around the shore,
and up a gully, after a good deal of scrambling and bad language. We
tied ourselves on to bushes and endeavoured to get some sleep; the
reason of fastening on like this was to stop ourselves rolling off the
peninsula. Next day we took over the trenches from a naval division;
they were not too keen on the trench fighting and did not do much
shooting. The enemy were very careless in exposing themselves and
enabled us to get a good shot or two. The furthest trenches are about
300 yards away and in some places the enemy's trenches are from 15 to
30 yards apart; the greatest danger in these close trenches are bombs
(they are devilish things too). The trenches we occupy are within 30 to
50 yards of the enemy's trenches.
  Most of the dead have been pulled away under cover of darkness.
Some who are lying too far out have been set on fire, by means of a
blazing rag thrown or poked out on to them. I suppose we have seen
our fair share of the horrors of war even if we have done no fighting. I
think I can say I have seen sights here that one does not get the chance

to see every day and, in fact, does not wish to see, i.e. the sinking of HMS *Triumph* and an Indian being flogged for thieving a watch. The two attacks I mentioned, of course, are not all that take place; lower down the coast they are always at it. After putting in thirteen days in the trenches we went down to the beach for a fortnight. They call it the Rest Camp; one works harder there than in the trenches, but we are never worked to death wherever we are. Poor old Bert Bailey's grave is about 10 yards from the seashore.

We lost Mr Cameron and Tas Smith on an outpost and a number of other good chaps. We were cut off and practically surrounded by thousands of Turks. There were only 98 of us when we took it over. It was a very trying 24 hours in a trench 3 feet deep and a foot to 18 inches wide. Eventually we were relieved by some other squadrons who fought their way through to us and covered our retreat with the wounded. If the Turks had have had any pluck at all none of us would have been alive today; they only had to swarm over the tops of the trenches and we would have been beaten by their numbers. They threw a good number of bombs in to us and caused a lot of damage. The means of dealing with these damnable things is to get a greatcoat over them to stop the force of the explosion — or to throw them out. The latter mode is rather dangerous.

Bert Green and another chap threw thirteen bombs back to the Turks. Mr Cameron was killed by a rifle bullet through the head; he was standing speaking to me at the time.

The whole of the 24 hours was put in on our knees. It was an awful job getting the wounded to a small space where we could lay them; we had to drag some of the poor beggars down the trench on their stomachs or backs. Tas Smith was blown up in the groin and stomach, and his legs were badly cut about; he died a very hard death and was in great pain . . .

The sunset effects here are fine, she sets behind two islands. There is an ideal climate here. So far we have had half a day's rain only, and it's warm at nights. The only signs of life I've seen here are an odd snake, a tortoise and a few centipedes and rabbits. Mat Dunn and Jack Dunn are quite well, both have had a touch of pneumonia. I had a letter from Jack O'Kaine and one from Bruce.

I met Len Noonan here, he has been away a while with a shrapnel wound in his head, but is quite all right now.

The flies here are a curse; they argue for every bite one eats. We get half a loaf of bread per man every second day and two spoonfuls of lime juice three times a week. Rum used to be issued to us every night, now we only get it on special occasions or when sapping. Didn't it cause some ill feeling too! We didn't half rouse. People seem to think that it's socks we want; in fact, we're overstocked with them. It's handkerchiefs that's needed, and an odd cake or two of chocolate. W. Nicholls, Didd Hill and Geo. Gillanders are well. Walley wished to be remembered to all.

The Turkish prisoners and dead are not too well clad, some of them wear pieces of goat's skin sewn to cloth for boots. Their footgear is exceptionally bad, so if we can get them on the run we'll have them footsore and beat them in two or three days.

The Maoris are attached to the Mounteds. Five or six of them have been caught by shrapnel and wounded. The Power boys are doing all right. Moses is not a sergeant, there is another Broughton here. The country about here has changed its aspect; where there was green scrub it is all dugouts and sleeping terraces. Where there is not much fear of shrapnel we all sleep in one big bed on a terrace. This is rather a pretty place, what I've seen of it, green, scrub-covered hills. The scrub is a broad-leaf plant. Some different classes are like holly, there are some stunted firs and sage grows handy — so we'll be able to season old Turkey well when we catch him. Poppies grow wild and very thickly. On our left flank there is a large plain and a lake; the plain is in a basin of the hills and is fronted by the sea. The plain is well cultivated and is studded with olive trees and a few dwellings. A large village is on the slope of the hills about four miles away. It gets its share of artillery and naval fire at times. There are very large cemeteries near this village, where the soldiers who fell in the Balkan War are buried. There is not much of a beach here, it's rather stoney, but the bays are very sandy-bottomed. Good bathing can be indulged in; that is, shrapnel and snipers permitting; the safest time is at night. When in the Rest Camp we manage a couple of swims a day and when in trenches one in every second day. We have not had a fresh-water wash since we lobbed here. Some of the fellows seem to get a good number of lice on themselves.

Water was scarce here at first and we had to manage on a little over a bottle a day; the ration is good now. Wood and water are our main troubles. The Turks used to keep up a tremendous rifle fire for about an hour three times a night; they seemed to be 'panicy'. One of their modes of firing is to throw the rifle on the top of the trench and blaze.

Their snipers are fine shots and one does not want to show oneself to any of these chaps for very long.

About the eighth day we were here they charged our trenches and suffered heavily. On a little piece of ground 300 dead were picked up and further down the line on 20 acres 3000 dead were buried.

They came first about midnight, were repulsed, and then came again before daylight. While charging they kicked up a Dickens of a row and called on Allah, but I don't think he stands to them too well. The British losses were very light. The enemy, about three days after this smack-up, asked for an armistice to bury the dead. This was granted and lasted from 9 a.m. to 4 p.m. Burying parties from both sides went out and carried on the business. It was a relief to our noses and tummys to have them buried. Some of the poor chaps had lain there three weeks, E.R. Wilson, the dentist, being amongst them. The trenches were swarming with maggots and flies. Another attack was delivered lately. There, losses were not so heavy.

Ralph Beetham is our lieutenant now. Our aeroplanes are pretty constantly on the move and drop an odd bomb or two; they draw a good deal of shrapnel fire but seem to dodge the shots. We see an odd Turkish plane, one dropped some papers one day, asking us to surrender and promised to treat us well, etc; very kind of them. We'll pay them a visit some day soon, I hope, as this living like a rabbit does not appeal to us. Troops here seem fairly healthy — the main sickness is diarrhoea and barked hands — I think it's flies that keeps them bad. If I can read the signs at all, methinks we won't see our horses for a space yet a while. We are being issued with infantry equipment. Everywhere we go we have to carry our gas helmets in case the blighters use gas. Short trousers are the fashion at Anzac Cove. There are some Sikh mountain battery men here; they are a fine-looking race, are scrupulously clean and good natured. The transport mule corps men are a weedier lot and not such good fellows. Our bill of fare is meagre and doesn't vary much — onions, potatoes, dried peas, haricot beans, bully beef, bacon, etc. and sometimes rice and prunes.

Well, Mum, the Regimental Censor (who, by the way, is Captain Spragg) will be getting tired of this long scrawl, so I had better cease fire with best of wishes to all and sundry.

I remain,
Your loving son
Will Harvey

44

P.S. Forgot to mention that a bullet scored my left shoulder on that outpost. It was a mere nothing. A bomb landed in our tucker box just where we were sitting down to lunch yesterday, nobody hurt. The tucker and tin suffered severely. Have had several letters lately. W.H.

A letter from William George Mayes (pictured). This letter was written from a hospital in Malta. William Mayes was in the original landing on Gallipoli. He was invalided out of the army in 1916 and died in New Zealand in 1959.

4 September 1915

Just a few lines to let you know that I am still alive and kicking. It is some time since I last wrote, but I haven't had a letter from you since May, and that was an old one. I put in a good four months' fighting, and on the 24th of August got bad, so they sent me to the hospital ship and this is where I ended. I think I have got what old Tua calls the 'rheumatic'. I can tell you that I am not sorry to have it; anything to get away from that hell. I didn't mind it while I was there, but, when you are away from the rattle of the rifles and shells, it makes one think of what one has gone through and things you have seen. I suppose you will know by the time you get this that 'Snowball' got a hit; it wasn't a bad one from what I could find out; only through the hand. Jim Melville, Dittmer and I were the only three from Rotorua that stuck it out the four months. Jim left two weeks before I did. Dittmer was there when I left. There were only seven of the old main body of the Haurakis that did any way over two months without getting hit or sick. I think the old saying is not far out, that it is better to be born lucky than rich, for I have had two bullets go through my cap and graze my head; one went through the sleeve of my shirt between the arm and body. One charge that I was in was like going through one of those big hailstorms that we used to get at Atiamuri. There were machine guns, rifles, and shrapnel; the air was quite warm, and you could smell the lead in it. One of these days the New Zealand people will know the way Bill Massey's tourists have been treated here. They and the Australians are the only troops that have been known to do four months in the firing line without a spell, and they are still there. I notice that anyone that has got away is not anxious to go back. One thing about them: they haven't been known to retire from a position they were to hold. The Tommies don't believe in holding on to the last man.

The author of this letter is unknown; however, he was a friend of Frank Bottle, who is mentioned in the missive. Frank Bottle survived the war and lived with a bullet in his neck until age 90. The photo shows a shell charge exploding near a ship during a battle at sea in the English Channel.

Salonika
4 January 1916

Dear Harry and all my chums
    At last I take the opportunity of dropping a line to you all. No doubt you are wondering where I am, and if I am still kicking. Well, old pals, I am still kicking, and getting three meals a day and a bed.

I would like to tell you a lot, but as you know, all our letters are censored, and one has to be careful nowadays. I do not feel inclined to tell you of my narrow escape from heaven or H— on the transport *Marquette* that was torpedoed on October 23rd, for we see so many letters that are exaggerated by some of the boys. Apart from that I will give you the truth and plain facts as regards to myself and Trooper Bottle, who resides at Hull Street, Oamaru.

Well, boys, we sailed from Alexandria on the ill-fated ship on October 19th, 1915. We had on board a detachment of the royal horses, artillery including 500 mules, and a large supply of ammunition, also the No. 1 Stationary Hospital with somewhere near 36 nurses. Our mess room was, at that time, in No. 2 hold astern, below the mules. Most of us came on deck every night to sleep, for the smell you could cut with a knife down below. Well, boys, all went well until the Friday (October 22nd). We had orders to mess in No. 2 hold forehead. Another two of my pals and myself again came on deck, but the sea became very rough, and a wave washed over the bow and drenched us, blankets and all. We then decided to go down to our old mess room, which was then vacant, and slept there. Of course, we were forbidden to strike a match, and what with the mules above us not being able to stand on their feet, and groans, well, we could not sleep. We were up early the next morning, went down for breakfast at 8 o'clock, and after that I was up on the saloon deck with some of the boys when, without any warning, an awful explosion took place, which shook the ship from end to end. We knew what had happened: a torpedo went right through our mess room, and caught some of the poor devils there. We all got our life belts and went round some of the boats, but after seeing the nurses on a lifeboat all ready to be lowered and all thrown into the sea, and another crashed on to another in the water, that was quite enough lifeboats for me. Well, I went along forehead, and there I saw the periscope of the submarine standing about 100 yards off, ready I suppose to give another if we did not sink, but there was no need.

It was there I met Trooper Bottle; he came up to me and we both took off our puttees and boots. By that time the ship was well under on one side and we were in the act of getting a piece of the hatches when she took another lurch and sent us into the winches. However, we crawled up the deck with a plank to the side which was high out of the water, when we heard a voice from the bridge shout, 'Jump for your lives, lads.' We didn't wait, I can tell you. After throwing the plank overboard, we dived in after it; I didn't know, boys, but I never felt the water, my mind was on the plank. Well, at last Bottle and myself got it. We would then be about 20 yards from the ship. We looked at the ill-fated boat, and one poor devil jumped off the stern and was cut to pieces on the propeller. The ship then took one huge dive and all was over. It was then I started to think of home and the good old times I used to have with the old chums on the cars. Then we heard a roar like thunder and it seemed like two tidal waves coming to meet us. I knew no more; till then I was gasping for breath. My pal, Bottle, was about 15 yards off me with the plank. It was, however, the escape of air from the ship below. It only lasted about one minute, but that was quite enough. Anyway, here we were in the water with nothing but wreckage, up-turned boats and cries and groans all round. The sea was by no means calm, but still, it could have been worse. I do not know how many times my pal and I were thrown over our plank by the waves. We were both hanging on like bulldogs to keep it level. Well, time passed on, boys, I began to think again of the good old times. After being about four hours in the water, we passed six poor devils dead in their life belts from exposure. We then noticed a lifeboat with about eight or nine in it about 20 yards off us. We called to them, but they took no notice. As time passed on, we began to feel the pinch, we were cold, shivering and could not feel our fingers even if we bit them. We then heard cheers from some rafts, and my mate said, 'Hang on, chum, we will be saved yet.' We could see two or three boats on the horizon, but it was in vain, they passed out of our sight. Well, by this time, we started to give up hope, as night was drawing in. I said to my mate, 'Can you hang on any longer?' He said, 'Not very long.' About another half hour, I tell you, my comrades, would have finished us both, when all of a sudden, my mate nearly lost his grip. He yelled to me, 'Hang on with all your might, we're saved.' I could then notice each time we got on top of the wave, that two ships were coming to rescue us.

The first to arrive was a French torpedo destroyer. From where I noticed her, she must have been a mile from us. Her lifeboats were picking up as many as they could. We were overjoyed, and all of a sudden, the HMS *Lynn* came direct to us — it was the happiest moment of my life, I can tell you. She came right alongside of us. The sailors on board seemed so eager to get us. They threw life buoys over to us, and when we got closer, they threw two ropes. I caught one and gave a piece to my mate. We heard one say, 'Hang on' and they started to pull us up, but we were just about done, and let go and dropped again into the water, and next thing I knew I was on board with all my clothes off and two Jack Tars pouring brandy into me. They gave me everything they could in the way of clothing, etc., and I owe my life to them. I have a scarf and a sea cap, which I wear to this day in memory of them.

From there we were transferred to the hospital ship *Grantully Castle*, an English ship, and we were treated like real k-nuts. They did everything for us. The doctor came round every morning to see us. He placed on my card 'slight pneumonia, diet light'. Of course, I planted it, and was living on the best.

France and the Western Front
–1916–

After the Anzac troops were withdrawn from Gallipoli in December 1915, the New Zealanders returned to Egypt, where a considerable reorganisation occurred. The Gallipoli veterans linked up with the newly formed Rifle Brigade, whose 1st Battalion had recently been in action against Senussi tribesmen. The arrival of the 7th, 8th and 9th Reinforcements meant it was possible to form an infantry division made up entirely of New Zealanders. For the first time in its history New Zealand had a complete infantry division abroad on active service.

Almost immediately upon its formation the New Zealand Division embarked for service on the Western Front, the decisive theatre of war for the British and Dominion armies. The New Zealanders landed at Marseilles in April of 1916, arriving to green hills and fields in glorious spring weather. Left behind in the sand and heat of Egypt was the bulk of the New Zealand Mounted Rifles, who would fight a different war during the Sinai-Palestine campaigns. There was little time for the New Zealanders to admire the charms of this new country, as the men were marched straight from the Marseilles docks to awaiting trains for shipment to the front.

When the New Zealand Division arrived in France in April 1916 it was not an effective fighting formation. The division was inexperienced and only partially trained. To use an American military term, the New Zealand Division in early 1916 was 'green'. While the original New Zealand infantry brigade had been well tested, the 2nd New Zealand Infantry Brigade was just two months old when it landed in France. It would be committed to the trenches in late May, barely three months after its formation. The learning curve for this brigade would be very steep indeed. The New Zealand Rifle Brigade had only come together as the division was leaving Egypt. It was so inexperienced

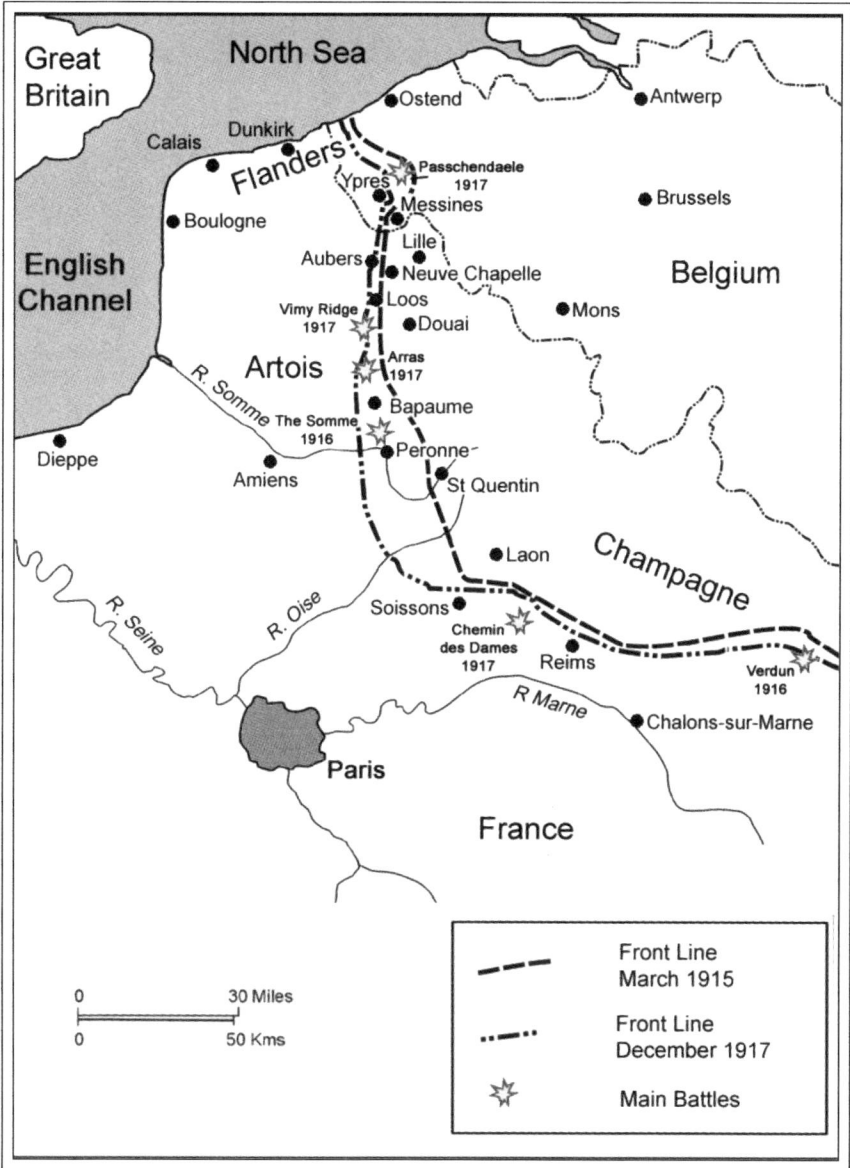

Great Britain

North Sea

●Ostend

●Antwerp

Calais

Dunkirk

Flanders

Ypres ▲Passchendaele
1917
●Messines

●Brussels

●Boulogne

Lille

Aubers ●●Neuve Chapelle

Belgium

English Channel

Loos
Vimy Ridge ● ●Douai
1917 ☆

●Mons

R. Somme

Artois

☆Arras
1917

●Bapaume

The Somme ●Peronne
1916 ☆

Dieppe

Amiens

●St Quentin

●Laon

Champagne

R. Seine

R. Oise

Soissons●

Chemin ☆
des Dames
1917

Reims●

Verdun ▲
1916

R Marne

●Chalons-sur-Marne

Paris

France

	Front Line March 1915
	Front Line December 1917
☆	Main Battles

| 0 | 30 Miles |
| 0 | 50 Kms |

that its first tour in the front-line trenches was cut short so that the riflemen could spend more time in training and in acquiring the most basic of soldier skills.

The Western Front was where the British Army made its main effort of the war, and it was ultimately where the war was won and lost. From the time of their arrival, the New Zealanders would be part of the bloody attritional struggles here, and they would be involved in nearly all the major battles connected with the British Army on the Western Front. The images that emerged from this struggle continue to haunt many people to this day. For the majority of people, this war is symbolised by the trenches of the Western Front and the great attritional battles needed to break these trench systems. This is so, not least because Britain and her Empire lost nearly one million dead in this war, most of them killed on the Western Front. Of New Zealand's casualties in the war of 1914–18, 84 per cent were experienced in the trenches of France.

The New Zealand Division was initially committed to a quiet sector of the front at Armentières. The area was regarded as a nursery and was used for the blooding of new divisions arriving in France. Armentières was also a location where the 'live and let live' system functioned. The advice many of the New Zealand soldiers received from their British counterparts on arriving there was, 'Don't fire at him, chum, and he won't fire at you.' Despite their inexperience, the New Zealanders were having none of this. They spent considerable time in repairing the trenches about Armentières, which had been allowed to fall in to disrepair, and began actively patrolling no-man's-land. They conducted much reconnaissance so that they became familiar with their frontage and fired on the Germans whenever they could. They also initiated several trench raids that took POWs and did much damage. As a result, the quiet nursery of Armentières soon warmed up considerably. At Armentières in those first few months in the front line, the New Zealanders established the routines that they would carry with them throughout their time in France. In the process, a raw, inexperienced division began its transformation into an effective fighting formation.

The main action of 1916 was the battle of the Somme, to which the New Zealanders were committed in its third phase. The battle of the Somme was the first real test for the New Zealand Division. On 15 September 1916, the same day that the newly invented tank made its appearance, the New Zealand Division attacked the German front-line trenches, along with nine other British divisions. The New Zealand attack occurred between High and Delville woods in the direction of Flers village. Ahead of them were three intact, formidable German trench systems.

In its attack on the Somme, the New Zealand Division took all its objectives and was in the line for three solid weeks from 15 September until 2 October 1916. This was the longest unbroken spell of any division during this phase of the battle. The New Zealand division stayed in line because of its efficiency in reducing the German positions and it stayed in the trenches, attacking again and again, until it was exhausted. When the New Zealanders were eventually withdrawn the division was in a sorry state. The men were spent, having reached the limits of their endurance. They were caked in mud, unshaven, their clothes were ruined and they had the appearance of walking skeletons. The casualties on the Somme had been very heavy, numbering 7408, the equivalent of seven of the division's 12 infantry battalions. Some units suffered losses in excess of 80 per cent of their personnel. The New Zealand Division had advanced some 3.2 kilometres through the German trenches. These hard-won gains showed the calibre of the New Zealand Division, especially that of its soldiers and junior officers.

There are nine letters in this section. One letter describes a trench raid in some detail, while the other letters relate directly to the battle of the Somme. Many of these letters are a powerful reminder of the cost of this battle for New Zealand. While the New Zealand Division passed its first great test of the war, and in doing so established a formidable reputation, this success came with a very high price tag. It would be many months before the New Zealand Division was in a fit state to be committed to a major action again.

Laurence Thaxter (pictured) describes in his letter an early trench raid. The last line of this letter is very poignant, as Thaxter never returned to New Zealand. He was killed by a German sniper on 15 October 1916.

*In Billets
Somewhere in France
3 July*

Dear May

It is over at last and I came out lucky again — just a small piece of bomb under the right eye, not bad enough to send me to hospital. The eye is completely bunged up, just as if someone had hit me in the eye. I had to go to a 'dressing station' to get the piece extracted and had my head bandaged up and they took my number and name, so I suppose my name will be on the casualty list again. I'm sorry if it is, for it will have caused a lot of worry at home, because I know the Defence people very well — they would inform you that I was wounded and leave you to guess how serious it was. I hope Mother has not been worrying about me. I only wish it had been a bit more serious so I could have got out of this altogether. I had a fair sickener of war last night. I will try and give you a few details of what happened. We collected in our front trench and waited until the appointed time (10.55 p.m.) to crawl out into no-man's-land and there wait while the bombardment was on.

No-man's-land is the ground between our trench and the enemy, about 150 yards across in this place. The time arrived, and we started to creep out in our sections, there were about a hundred of us and the time allowed us to get to the middle of no-man's-land was ten minutes. When the ten minutes were up, the artillery were going to start shelling the German trench. There were twenty-five men behind me; I crawled through the drain under our trench and I had no sooner got outside when the artillery started. It was such a mess-up, we had about 80 yards to go to the middle of no-man's-land before we could consider ourselves safe. The first batch of shells had hardly exploded before the Germans sent up hundreds of star shells and also had a searchlight playing over the ground; then their artillery got going. Such a picnic! There we were, all crawling through the grass, lying down as flat as we could whenever a star shell came over us, and as soon as the light died down going like mad again. It was a trying time, shells and French mortar bombs bursting all around us. Every now and then someone would roll over with a sickening groan. We got out at last and some managed to get into shell holes, some in a creek, and others (myself among them) struck a shallow tunnel that had been blown in and forgotten months before. It was a most welcome shelter — a shell would have blown it in and caught the lot of us, but all the same it was good protection from flying fragments. The bombardment of the German trench was to continue for 20 minutes; after that, the guns were going to lift and shell the second line about 60 yards back. As soon as that happened we were going to rush the first trench, kill or take prisoner everyone in it and at the expiration of 15 minutes withdraw again to our own line. We waited and as soon as the guns lifted our wire-cutters rushed forward and cleared a gap through the wire entanglement for us to pass through. While they were doing that we formed up in our proper sections and were all ready when the order came to advance. We placed our scaling ladders across the drain and climbed into the trench, I climbed on to the back of the trench and looked about and discovered a bay in the trench 15 yards ahead. I gave the order to bomb it and as I did so I heard several soft thuds — it was bombs falling around me. I lost no time in throwing myself face downwards. They went off without doing me any damage, but others had landed among my mates in the trench and I am sorry to say they were not as lucky as I was. Those bombs were what we call 'smoke bombs', they filled the trench with a thick white smoke and I could not see a hand's breadth in front of me. I had no idea how my mates had fared or where they had got to. I scrambled to my feet and took a few steps forward when 'thud, thud'. I heard some more dropping. I dropped too. I must have laid alongside of one, for my rifle was blown out of my hand and the seat out of my pants and I was rolled over into the trench. As I laid there trying to collect my wits another bomb exploded close to my head. I received concussion and a splinter under the right eye; it temporarily blinded me in both eyes. I thought I was done for. I climbed out of the trench, was guided across the ladders and through the gap in the wire and started to make my way back as well as I could. I wandered about on no-man's-land, and eventually found myself on an old metal road. I heard a machine gun rattle and heard the whish, whish of bullets. I dived headlong into the grass on the left-hand side of the road, laid quiet for a few minutes, then commenced to crawl to the left, which I knew was the direction of our trenches. After crawling about for a few minutes I struck a track through the grass that led me to a shell hole and the shell hole was the entrance to the tunnel that we had taken shelter in before. You've no idea how I blessed the maker of that tunnel. I cannot describe what my feelings were, blind as a bat, crawling about in the grass under machine gun and artillery fire. Several others soon joined me in the tunnel, and in the dark the sight of my left eye gradually came back. We started to explore the tunnel but it twisted and turned about so much that we lost all sense of our direction, and when we came to where it was caved in and saw the parapet of a trench about 30 yards ahead, we did not know whether it was our own or the Germans', so sorrowfully turned back to our starting point, there to wait until the bombardment ceased. We waited there for close on two hours. Our party had increased to about 20, mostly wounded, by that time and when we did start to crawl home it was a long job as we all had to help one another, but we got there at the finish, and it was a very tired, weary, old Laurie that turned up at the billet at 4 a.m. I had been reported missing, someone had seen me rolled over into the trench and thought that was the end of me. We lost some fine men that night and a good many were wounded. It's not for me to criticise the night's work so all I will say is that the men acted splendidly under unforeseen and almost insurmountable difficulties, and the officers, too.

I am sorry to say that I never got a souvenir or even saw a sign of 'Minenwerfer', but she shook me up several times as I lay out in no-man's-land. That's all about that little game. I received a couple of postcards (in an envelope) from you and today I got one of the parcels Mum sent, one with biscuits, dates, raisins, chocs, cocoa, coffee, jam etc. I am slightly off my tucker (effects of shell shock) but my mates did justice to the nice things, and all send their thanks. Will have to close now. Give my kind regards to Mrs Allen and family and also to Mrs Waller, and don't let Mum worry about me and don't you worry either; remember, I promised to be home for Christmas and I think I will be too. Give my love to Mum and Chris and Syd. Heaps of love and kisses for yourself (I wish I were near enough to deliver them personally).

Laurie

P.S. am sending my 'farewell' letter for you to read, it will explain a few details and save me a lot of writing. By Jove, it was nearly my farewell letter all right. I came out better than I expected. I hope I have the same luck next time.

Laurie

❦

Edwin Farrell (pictured right) won a Military Medal for his gallantry on the Somme in 1916. A Gallipoli veteran, Edwin Farrell spent considerable time convalescing in Egypt and England from wounds received there before joining the New Zealand machine gunners in France in 1916. Captain Farrell returned to New Zealand and died in 1977.

On Somme Front, France
9 October 1916

Dear Mother

You will no doubt be wondering at my long silence, but during the past month we have been too busy with other things to think of writing.

You will know long ere this letter reaches you all about our doings of the past three weeks. Perhaps you will know now, more than we do, of what the New Zealand Division has done on the Somme front. I can hardly realise, even now, miles back from the firing line, that I have got safely through those few weeks with nothing more than a few good frights and a bit of skin off my left shoulder.

Needless to say, I have had extraordinary luck. Our Company started with two full teams and two machine guns in charge of a sergeant. That is thirteen men. Well, my gun got a shell through it and we came out with just a full team for the remaining gun. We were reinforced by another gun and full team from headquarters. When we came out last time after our stunt 'over the parapet', the sergeant brought out one gun and I brought the other, we two being the sole survivors of the last two teams. So you can see by that we have had a fairly interesting time during our spell on this front.

As you know, by previous letters, we worked up towards the Somme by easy marches from one village to another. We finally arrived at a camp close by the trenches from which the big push started on the 1st July. Here we spent a few days, doing nothing in particular. Our next move was the evening before the push of September 15. That night we camped in the famous Nametz Wood and snatched what sleep we could, for the continual banging of guns was anything but peaceful.

All next day, until about 3 p.m., we lay in the wood and then we moved forward. Our new position was in a trench from which we could view the ridge over which the Rifle Brigade charged that morning. High Wood was on the left of it and the famous Delville Wood was visible away on the right. After dark we moved up into the trench from which the Dinkums [nickname of the Rifle Brigade] started out. Next morning we received orders to go forward to Flers, the village which the 'Dinks' and 141st London Terriers had taken the previous day.

We moved forward over the ridge in artillery formation. We were no sooner on the skyline than Fritz opened up on us with his 5.9 guns, using high explosive. For the next 800 yards we experienced as heavy a shell fire as ever any of us could have thought of in our wildest dream. It was two or three Hells run all into one. However, all bad things come to an end. We finally reached a trench and had a much needed spell.

We were supposed to go over the top at 1.30, but only Wellington went forward, taking part of a 'communication trench' with hardly any opposition. In the evening we filed into this trench. While waiting in this trench for orders, a shell knocked my machine gun to pieces, but did not harm any of the crew. After dark our Company filed out of the trench in the direction of Flers village, which was on our right. Taking up a line, we commenced to dig in, thus connecting up with a portion of trench running along in front of Flers. By this move, Flers was made secure from attack on the left front and flank. Except for a few flares and a few rounds from a machine gun, we were allowed to dig in undisturbed — very much to our surprise and relief.

Next day was spent improving our trench. A few shells landed near us, but not enough to worry us much. Fritz's trench was 800 yards away, running along a ridge in front of Gouzeaucourt and to say the very least, it was getting a very, very, unhappy time. Our shells were bursting in and around it in a ceaseless stream. That night we had a fairly lively time, for we were expecting Fritz to counterattack. Which he did — twice, but not on our sector of trench. However, both attempts were of a very feeble nature and were easily beaten off, only a few bombs being thrown on each occasion.

Our source of annoyance was two batteries of 'whizz bangs' which Fritz brought up close to us under cover of darkness. These guns played shrapnel up and down our trench all night, causing us to watch ceaselessly for an infantry attack and also knocking a number of our men out of action. The shooting of these guns was the most beautiful that I have yet seen. Almost every shell burst just in front or over our parapet, the shrapnel raining into the parados behind us.

Morning seemed as if it would never come, but at last the welcome dawn broke and then shells ceased, for the batteries had to withdraw. All this day it kept raining and you can imagine what a mess the newly dug trench was in by night, and of course we were all soaked to the skin, for 'fighting order' consists of only web equipment, our ordinary uniform and a groundsheet.

We started the march back to the reserve trenches — a march that I will never forget as long as I live, for the ground was sodden with rain and pitted with shell holes full of mud, as close together as it was possible to stick them. We were hardly a couple of hundred yards away from the trench when Fritz opened upon the ridge we were crossing with a battery of 5.9s. A number of shells landed very near us and a man was killed beside me. Pieces flew all round me, but my luck was out and none hit me. To make a long story short, we staggered up to our reserve trench three hours after starting. The cooks had a hot meal ready for us and we did it justice, you may be sure.

After the meal we filed into the trench to find dugouts, but our luck was still out, for we machine gunners found there were no bivvies for us, so we had to stand beside a miserable fire, in the rain, and wait for daylight. The weather was very cold and that did not add to our comfort by any means. Day broke at last and we then set about making bivvies for ourselves. A very miserable job too, for there was mud everywhere. A few days later the weather cleared and the ground dried and we then began to enjoy ourselves once more.

On the 24th of September in the evening our brigade again moved forward to the front and support trenches, the 1st and 2nd

Companies of our battalion taking up their positions for the attack on the following day and the 12th and 13th Companies taking up their positions in reserve. Our Company (the 12th) filed into a trench. At least, it was called a trench by the officer who showed it to us. To me it looked more like a heap of loose earth along the remains of a hedge. And the ground fairly stank of high explosives. Well, we dug holes in the bank here and there to put our heads in, for it was a hopeless task trying to make a trench in the loose earth. I predicted to my mates that the following day (the 25th) was going to be the worst we had ever experienced in our lives and I was right.

As soon as dawn broke the shells — big ones — began to fall around our heap of dirt and this continued all day, burying men time after time and causing many casualties in our already well thinned ranks. At 12.35 the 1st and 2nd Companies went over the parapet and then we in this trench went through all the different kinds of Hell that were ever thought of. Dante's Inferno was a Heaven beside it. The reason was that Fritz dropped his barrage on the ridge which our trench was on. It was during this time that a young lad, my No. 2 on the gun, and as good a mate as a man ever had, was killed beside me. Poor little beggar, we had been joking a few minutes before about him going on leave to his home in England this month. He would have been 21 on the 4th of this month if he had lived.

About 4 p.m. we received orders to retire to a sunken road in Flers village. We had to run the gauntlet for about 400 yards, but excepting for two men who were buried and suffocated before we could dig them out, we all managed the journey safely — and in pretty quick time, too. Our casualties in the machine gunners up to now were a gun knocked out and six men — a full team — during the first spell in from 16 to 18 September. On 25 September we lost another full team, leaving us with two guns and six trained men. We lay in reserve in the Sunken Road all of 26 September and most of the time heavy shells were falling around it, for the Huns knew it was being used for a dressing station and headquarters, etc. I had my dugout blown in on top of me, the gun buried and a lot of my magazines and ammunition went up in smoke, but our position was weakly held, there being only about one man to every four or five yards.

We spent an anxious night waiting for Fritz to attack. All the same, we had our sleep as usual and even if the Germans had paid us a visit, we would have given them 'a father of a hiding'.

The following night the 2nd Brigade relieved us. The sergeant now had one gun, we being the only two left out of over twenty men. Just when we were leaving the trench one of our own shells exploded near to us. A chap beside me was hit through the stomach and a junk got me in the shoulder, but my luck was still out, for the lump was too big to penetrate my web equipment. I had a rotten time that night carrying the gun home, but I eventually got it there. Two days later the Company returned to the reserve trenches behind Flers, but as my shoulder was stiff I remained with the cooks until they came out again.

With the same shell my equipment was also blown to shreds. This I would not have minded so much had not my haversack gone up in smoke with it. The haversack contained my emergency rations, which were composed of a couple of tins of fancy biscuits, a tin of tongues and two tins of Ideal Milk — things which it was impossible to buy within fifteen or twenty miles of Flers village.

During the night we were kept busy carrying rations, bombs, ammunition, etc. to the firing line, which had been pushed forward almost a mile by our 1st and 2nd Companies. They took their objectives, Factory Corner, and dug in about 50 yards on the far side of the buildings. Their casualties, for the amount of ground taken, were remarkably small, each Company having less than ten slightly wounded.

The following day we lay in the Sunken Road. In the evening we took up rations, etc. again and then went up ourselves, taking up our position in the front trenches from which we were to attack the following day. We dug most of the night and went to sleep at dawn. I was roused at 1 p.m. and told to get the gun prepared for moving. We had to file along the trench about 300 yards to get into our correct position, as this trench was already occupied by men who were to form the first wave in the attack. We had very little room, for the trench was only about fifteen to eighteen inches wide. Fritz must have observed us, for we were no sooner in position than eight-inch shells began to fall all around us. We had a quarter of an hour to wait before the attack and it seemed as if we would all be blown to bits before we received the word to advance. At 2.15 p.m. the guns opened the shrapnel barrage on Fritz's trench and our first line, or wave, hopped over the parapet and began their stroll across no-man's-land, followed at a distance of 40 yards by the second wave, with which I and the gun went, on the right flank. The noise from the bursting shells of the barrage was terrific and to me it seemed as though all the tin pots and pans in Hell were clanging around my ears. I did not have much time to think, however. Fritz began to put up a stubborn fight just in front of us, holding up our first wave in his barbed wire. Here my gun came into play. Dodging from shell hole to shell hole, I managed to get about 15 yards off the trench inside the barbed wire. By this time my team was reduced to a wounded man and myself, the rest of them having been killed beside me on the way over. From the position which I held, I could put an enfilade fire along the portion of trench from which the Germans were firing and throwing their bombs. After I had divided about 300 rounds amongst them, very few of them remained and these few, thinking no doubt that discretion was better than valour, made a dash for the ridge behind. However, they never reached it. On one small track my gun had a heap of over forty lying and those who did not use the track were very hospitably attended to by the men with rifles. I saw only three reach the ridge and cross it, but how they would get on afterwards is doubtful, for our guns were raining shrapnel on the far side of that ridge.

We dug in under the skyline of this ridge for two more days in reserve and we shook the Somme mud from our boots. Entraining at Albert, we railed to Longpré. We spent four good days at this town and then went on to Caestre, travelling from that town to Estaires in motor lorries. From Estaires we marched to Sailly and we have been there ever since. The largest town thereabouts is Levanter. Our billet is only five minutes' walk from Levanter, so we usually go in there every night. I left France on leave on the 3rd December and will be going back on the 14th. So far I have had the time of my life.

Now I am with the Reeds and having the time of my life. They cannot do enough for me. The girls (four) are just delicious and I suppose if I was Herbert instead of Ed, I would have been engaged to one long ere this. However, there's plenty of time after the war.

With the very fondest of love and best of kisses,
I remain,
Your ever loving son
Edwin

❊

One of the casualties on the Somme was Lieutenant Fred McKee (pictured), whose letter on the Gallipoli campaign appears on pages 25–36. The family received two letters from his fellow soldiers. This one is from his platoon sergeant.

France
26 October 1916

MR MCKEE

Dear Sir

It is with very great regret that I am writing these few lines in connection with your son Lieutenant McKee's death and as I was with him at the time of his death I feel it is my duty to express my feelings of regret at losing such a valuable officer and one that is so dear to you.

It was on the night of the 21st September our battalion went over the top to take a strong position held by the enemy and as I was in the same platoon as he, and being held in reserve for special duties with your son, several others and I were told to go and bomb a trench. We all were on our way over with our load of bombs when we were seen by the Germans — immediately their machine guns and rifles opened fire on us. Your son very bravely got the rest of the party to take shelter in a shell hole and while doing this he was shot through the head and died almost instantaneously. We tried our best to save him by doing what we could for him but he was unconscious all the time till he passed away

63

only a few minutes after being hit. I can assure you we in his platoon send our heartfelt sympathy to you in your great loss of such a brave soldier, as he was always very popular with the boys indeed for his kindness and thoughtfulness, as well as being one of the most plucky officers we have and now he is gone you can only say he has done his duty through and through and served his King and country for the great cause, Liberty.

You and your family have the very deepest sympathy of the Company and my fellow NCOs.

I remain Yours
Sergeant V. G. Hunter
12 Nelson Company

The other letter received by the McKee family was from Brigadier 'Bill' Braithwaite, Lieutenant McKee's brigade commander.

New Zealand Reserve Camp
Sling Camp
Salisbury Plain
England
26 November 1916

Dear Sir

Ever since your son's death I have been intending to write to you, but I have been laid up myself and unable to do so.

I would like to tell you how much I sympathise with you and your family in your great sorrow, and I can only hope that your grief may be lightened by the knowledge that your son died a glorious death for his King and his country.

He is a great loss to this brigade and to the 2nd Canterbury Battalion in particular. I knew him very well. He was a first-class officer. The pages of history do not contain a more glorious story than the work of the 2nd Canterbury Battalion on the Somme between 15th September and 2nd October 1916. I feel sure that Colonel Stewart and his brother officers will also have written to you.

I am over in England for a short time and rejoin my brigade next month.

With my deepest sympathy. Please forgive me for not having written before.

I am

Yours very sincerely

W. G. Braithwaite

Brigadier-General

Commanding 2nd New Zealand Brigade

New Zealand Division

France

∞

This letter was written by Private Hector McLeod (pictured, fourth from the right). Hector served in Egypt, Gallipoli and France. After his wounding on the Somme, Hector was offered the chance to return to New Zealand but chose to stay in England, so that he could recover and return to his mates.

It proved a fateful choice. Private Hector McLeod was killed at Passchendaele nearly a year after writing this letter.

24 September 1916

Dear Mollie

Just a line to say that I am keeping well although wounded. I was hit in the back of the neck by a piece of high explosive shell while advancing at the Somme.

I was knocked completely out. When I came to I did not know

where I was for some time. I could not move, as I was half buried and my head was ringing some. At last I got myself out and took off my gear and made for the rear. I passed some of my mates — dead — while going back. I had my wound dressed and made off to the nearest dressing station about two miles off. I was about done when I got there. My wound was properly dressed and I was sent off in a motor car to No. 1 General Hospital Rheon. I was there for a night and then sent to Blighty, where I am now. I met Jack Kennedy making for the front line as I was coming away, he is in the 2nd Brigade. I have not heard how any of the Mosgiel boys got on yet — a casualty list of the New Zealanders has not been printed yet. It will be some time, as we advanced over a lot of ground. You would not know that there had been any trenches at all where we advanced, as we could see nothing but shell holes with German dead everywhere. The Germans got in these shell holes with machine guns and bombs and mowed our men down. When we got to them, they threw up their hands and cried for mercy, but we gave them the bayonets. Our shells burst their liquid-fire cylinders and they were burnt to blazes themselves. It was pitiful to see some of them. It's nothing to face the Germans hand to hand, it's the getting to them through the artillery fire. This is not war, it's absolute murder. The peninsular was a home to over there. Armentières was bad enough, but nothing to the Somme. They say the Somme fighting is worse than the fighting at Verdun was, so you will just have a slight idea what it is like. The Mosgiel boys that were wounded at Armentières can thank their stars that they were not in the big push at the Somme. I was hit on the 16th of September and am still in bed but can walk out to have a wash. The nurses will not let us walk about till our wounds are fairly healed, so when I get better I will go to see Auntie; I have written to her. Well, Mollie, I have not much news to tell. Do not worry about me, mine is only a scratch compared to some of the boys and I am doing tip-top. You will say that yourself when you see me coming home, and it won't be long either. The Germans have had about enough of it. Well, Mollie old girl, I will bring it to a close this time. With heaps of love and kisses from your ever-loving brother Hector.

P.S. Remember love to all and Jim.

H. M.

No.1 General Hospital
Brockenhurst
England

In this letter, Private W.M. Innes writes to the father of a close friend killed on the Somme. The letter contains details of the death of Private Harold Lagor Beach, who was killed in action on 16 September 1916, aged 22. The letter is unusual in that pulls no punches in describing the circumstances of Private Beach's death. It also describes in graphic detail the circumstances of the writer's own wounding in that terrible battle. This letter is from the Kippenberger Military Archive and Research Library Waiouru (1989.860).The above photo is of an advanced dressing station, and was taken during the battle of Messines. Though the location differs from that referred to in the following letter, the conditions would have been similar.

No. 3 Southern General Hospital
Codford
England
24 October 1916

My Dear Mr Beach

I suppose you will be surprised to hear from me, but no doubt you will be looking forward to a letter from some of us boys to hear of poor old Harold, my mate. I suppose you will know long before this letter reaches you that Harold died of wounds on the Somme. He got hit the first morning we went over the top and he lay out all that day and the next night. The stretcher-bearers found him next morning at dawn. It was impossible to get at the wounded in the daylight and they were very hard to find at night as all the land was new to the bearers. They could only find the wounded by their groans and some of the poor fellows were never found until it was too late and they were either dead or would die as soon as they moved them. Just the same as in Harold's case. I never saw Harold while he was conscious after he got hit, but I think he must have known that he was done, as when they brought him to the dressing station he asked for me, if I was still alive and if he could see me. They sent for me, but we had advanced about 1_ miles the day before past our dressing station and by the time I got the message and got back, poor Harold was unconscious and had been for about half an hour. I was very sorry indeed, as I would have very much like to have spoken to him before he died. He passed away soon after I got there and he is buried with the rest of our boys in a town we had taken called Flers (you may have seen it on the map) and I think, Mr Beach, it was a godsend when he died as, poor fellow, he must of suffered awful and I think you would have said the same if you had seen him. A large piece of shell hit him just above the groin and it went right through him. The doctor said there was no hope for him as soon as he saw him and we can say that he could not have died more nobly and is at rest now.

Well, Mr Beach, I managed to keep going till 27 September, about ten days after Harold got his. We had just taken the Germans' third line on that date and eight of us bombers were preparing for a counterattack when a trench shell landed fair in the middle of us. It blew five to pieces and buried the other three of us. They got me out first, but the other two they could not find for a long while. I had been lying there after they dug me out for over an hour waiting for bearers and they had just come across one of them then, but he was dead. Of course, the shock may have killed him, as it sent me unconscious, and I think that it was just as well, for I came too just a few minutes before they got me out and, my God, I shall never forget them as long as I live . . .

My God, Mr Beach, a man is very lucky indeed to get out of the Somme alive. It was simply hell on earth. I suppose you will all know our losses there, but the boys can say that we advanced further than any other troops on that Somme front in that one advance. There was no stopping the boys when they got going . . .

Well, Mr Beach, you all have my deepest sympathy in the loss of dear old Harold, but you can proudly say that he died bravely fighting for his country. I shall miss him when I get back with the boys.

I will have to close now as I think I have told you all the news. Remember me to all your boys and I hope to see you again one of these days.

From your sincere friend

W. M Innes

P.S. I have Harold's two collar badges and I am sending you them as soon as I am able to get about.

✂

Letters of Cuthbert William Free, MC, of the Canterbury Infantry. The first letter describes his elation at the opportunity to lead a company in the forthcoming Somme battle. The second letter details his fate. 'Dame Fortune' did smile on Cuthbert Free, as he survived the war and saw service in Afghanistan. These letters are from a comprehensive collection housed in the Kippenberger Archive and Research Library at Waiouru (1998.882). The photograph shows a battalion of New Zealanders in full kit, and with handcarts, going out to take their spell of duty in the trenches during 1916.

10 September 1916

Dearest Mother

Two or three times in the last month or so I've tried to write to you, but have never got more than half a dozen lines done. Since we left Armentières I have seen half of France and done a certain amount of intensive training, which is to say going eyes out for as many hours as a man can stand. I enjoyed the trip through France immensely — did it on bicycle — a means of progression for which the road and the country generally are most wonderfully suited. It was so nice too, being a day ahead of the crowd and getting everything more or less *au naturel*. Truly the position of billeting officer is not without its delights.

But the greatest good news of all is yet to be told. I have a most wonderful knack of landing on my feet in the end, even though I do turn somersaults at times. In our next scrap, which is a matter of hours away, I am to lead the company. Owing to the nature of the fighting some officers are always left out of the big shows. Norman S. is out of this one and I am in. I was afraid I would be left and he taken, but Dame Fortune has smiled once more. I don't believe she's really so fickle as a good many people would suppose. She certainly has stuck to me in many things. At present I'm sitting among the saplings of what was once Fricourt Wood and the bombardment is just like a heavy sea on a rocky coast — it sounds like it, I mean. It certainly has considerably more effect.

I meant to have a photo taken for you when I was in Amiens, but I was only there for an hour, which I devoted to lunch and a bath. It's one of the drawbacks of billeting — being always one day or night ahead of the transport, one never sees a sign of his kit and in anything but the largest towns anything like a bath is unknown. I wonder if you remember me telling you of the Lincoln College dance held while we were in camp at Yaldhurst and how Jumbo Murchison, sitting in a collapsible bath, looked just like a big pink baby and reminded me of Pears' soap. He won't be happy till he gets thin. Well, I *felt* like that baby one morning in billets when I had taken advantage of the old dame's absence to have a bath in her kitchen. She came back and stood in the doorway and gazed in astonishment. '*Les Anglais, les Anglais, qu'ils sout fous* [sic],' she exclaimed as I squeezed the sponge down the back of my neck — and I believe she'd have sat down and started a conversation if I hadn't asked her if she'd oblige me by withdrawing. I honestly believe the peasant people never bath. If they do, I don't know how they manage it. And yet the houses, the kitchens, the linen (of which they are wonderfully proud — an old woman's face will glow with pleasure as she shows you the texture of your sheets which were part of her 'dot' fifty years ago — and it's all monogrammed) as I was saying, their houses are scrupulously clean and the courtyards etc, incredibly filthy.

Bye bye anon, the battalion cometh and I must meet it.

Ever

Cuthbert

Brockenhurst
25 September 1916

Dear Mother

Well, here I am in hospital, *hors de combat* for a while, I'm afraid. My total injuries are one large bruise, one hole in my chest where a shrapnel ball went in, and another where it came out after following the ribs round — which, of course, was better than going through my heart as it should have done only for the rib — and an awkward cut in the left hand which is going to take some time to get well — a piece of shrapnel tried to take my thumb off and nearly succeeded along the front of it. Fortunately, no bones are broken, no sinews cut — but the thing scooped up the nerves and the thumb feels neither hot nor cold now.

I have been here three days now, have got my kit from Cooks, seen Mrs Lemin (that's how it is spelt), heard from Les Wylde and the Everetts, and am bored to extinction already.

I went through the Somme stunt and Friday and Saturday, and got it Sunday night.

My chest is OK, but my hand is painful and a beastly encumbrance. When the bandages are less in size I'll write at length.

Hope you got my cable.

Cheer Ho.

Ever

Cuthbert

※

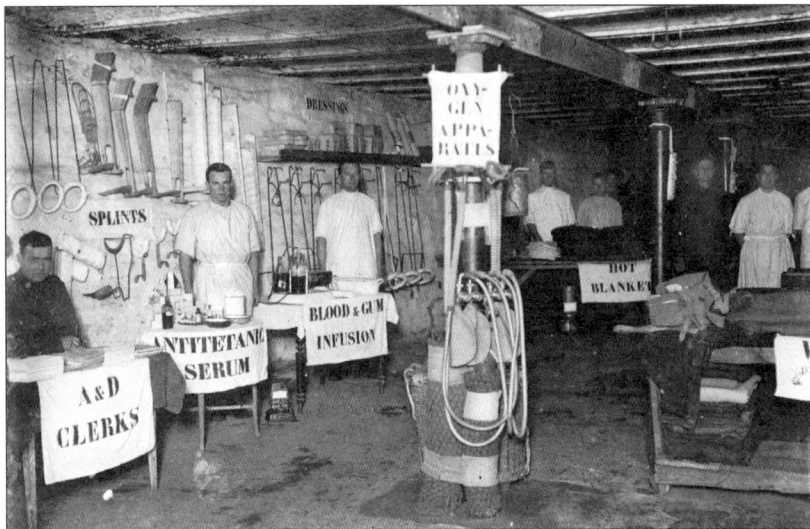

Gunner David Oliphant Stewart, a veteran of Gallipoli, writes here to his mother with details of his wounding on the Somme. Though he is writing from hospital in England, David Stewart would most likely have been first treated in a field hospital, similar to the one depicted above. This letter is from the Kippenberger Military Archive and Research Library, Waiouru (1998.1953).

New Zealand Hospital
Walton on Thames
19 September 1916

My Dear Mother

I expect that you will be getting official information in a week or so that I was wounded on the Somme. I have cabled to Ellen to say that I am convalescent, so I expect that she will receive my wire before the official announcement reaches you. I have only got a flesh wound in the side, which is nearly healed already, and I can get about all right though I expect I shall be a little stiff for a week or so. The shell which caught me burst about five yards away so that the piece that hit me had plenty of velocity to carry it right through, leaving a nice clean wound.

Our battery was just behind a place called Delville Wood, or Devil's Wood as the Tommys call it, a wood utterly devoid of foliage or any green and the trees blasted and broken and uprooted by shell fire. I am sorry that I was hit just before our concentrated attack on the

Germans, as I should like to have seen all our artillery at work at once, some thousands of heavy guns.

There were batteries of guns of various calibres as far as one could see with a pair of glasses and then the French artillery away to the right again firing day and night — and sounding in the distance like a tremendous storm on a rocky coast — great bursts and surges of sound. We were in the front of the other batteries in our part and had eighteen 18-pounders, quick-firing guns, about 30 yards immediately behind us and firing over our heads. At that distance the 18-pound gun has an ear-splitting crack and is far worse than any of the heavier guns in that respect being, I suppose, the noisiest gun in the army at close quarters, and as these were firing 10 to 15 rounds each per minute, night and day, during the time I was there, you can imagine the noise. Add to this the fact that they are using American shells, which are liable to burst almost at the muzzle of the gun and pepper everything in front, and you will see our position was no sinecure.

However, I am thankful to say my wound was from a German shell and not one of our own guns, as many others were. After a time, when one gets used to it, the sound of the guns, if not too close, has rather a soothing sound at night and I quite miss the noise in this quiet village. I expect to be shifted either today or tomorrow to a convalescent camp at either Brokenhurst in Hampshire or Hornchurch — both New Zealand establishments — where I will stop for a while and then hope to get a week or two furlough before returning to France for the winter.

Well, I must finish now as I have just been told to get ready to go to Codford near Salisbury.

With best love from
Your affectionate son
David O. Stewart

The Sinai-Palestine Campaign

A fter the Gallipoli campaign, the New Zealand Division was formed and sailed for France in early 1916. This was to be the country's main effort of the war. Left behind to fight a little known, unpublicised campaign in the deserts of Egypt and Palestine was the New Zealand Mounted Rifle Brigade, eventually about 3000 strong. Later, two additional companies of men were supplied for the Imperial Camel Corps, and a Wireless Corps was provided for service in Mesopotamia. During this long campaign, more than 17,000 New Zealanders served in Sinai-Palestine. A Boer War veteran, Brigadier Edward Chaytor, from Motueka, commanded the New Zealand Mounted Rifle (NZMR) Brigade. The brigade was part of the Anzac Mounted Division led by an outstanding Australian commander, Major General Harry Chauvel.

The Sinai-Palestine campaign was little more than a sideshow to the main theatre of war in France and Belgium. It was a place where hopes ran high for a cheap, easy victory over an enemy that was not highly regarded by the Allied leaders. Such hopes were to be cruelly dashed, as the war here dragged on and experienced an equal share of disasters before victory was finally achieved.

The terrain of the Middle East was very inhospitable for these new arrivals. As well as Turks and Germans, the soldiers had to battle searing heat during the day, freezing cold at night, sand, thirst, malaria, flies, kamsin (sandstorms), and a monotonous diet of bully beef and biscuits. It was the type of unpleasant campaigning that another generation of New Zealand soldiers would become so familiar with. Despite these discomforts, conditions here were infinitely better than those on the Western Front.

The progress of the campaign hinged on logistical supply, especially

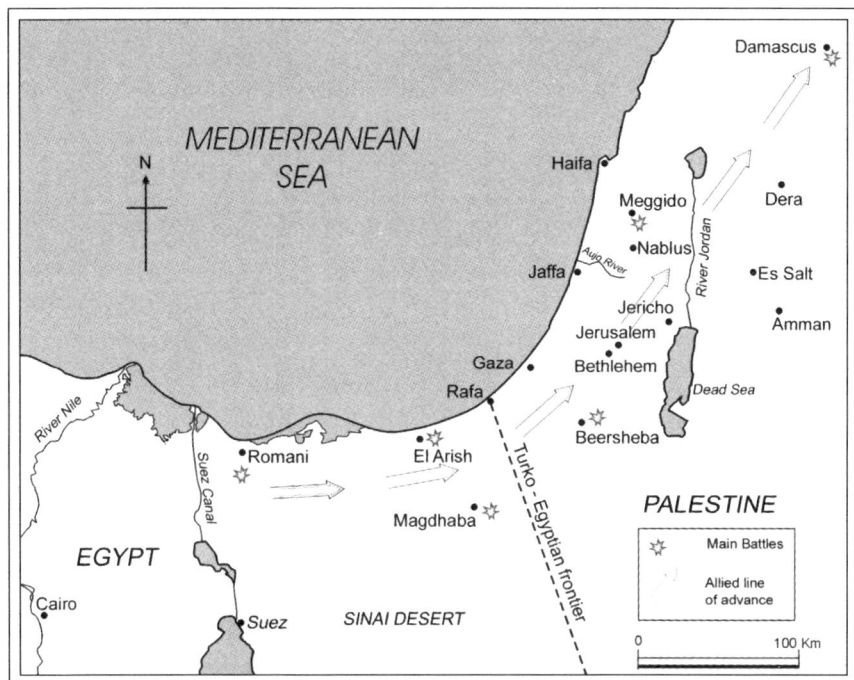

the availability of water for troops and horses. New Zealand horses during this campaign were renowned for being able to go for long periods without water — between 60 and 70 hours when really tested. The horses suffered the same privations as their masters during campaigning. In addition, they suffered from 'flu', ringworm, sand cholic and sores around the mouth and eyes caused by the ever-present flies. In all, New Zealand sent nearly 10,000 horses to this campaign and only one is known to have returned. At the end of the campaigning some of the New Zealand horses were kept for the Occupation Force, but most were shot, one of the hardest tasks New Zealand soldiers have ever had to perform. To make things easier, each squadron changed over their horses prior to the shootings. The dead horses, many with more battle scars than their owners, were left in rows along the Mediterranean shore.

The first action of the New Zealand Mounteds was in the vicinity of Romani, some 30 kilometres east of the Suez Canal. Sent there in April 1916 to patrol the desert, dig wells and report on Turkish movements, the New Zealanders proved adept at this style of warfare. The Turks responded to the build-up of troops and supplies at Romani, attacking it with 14,000 troops on 4 August 1916. The attack was anticipated and the British positions were well prepared. It was repulsed, with heavy losses for the Turks. About 5000 Turks were killed or wounded in this battle and a further 4000 captured over five days of fighting. As the Turks withdrew back across the desert, the Anzac Mounted Division pursued them.

The battle of Romani established a pattern that was to persist for much of the campaign. This pattern was one of coping with the trying conditions of the Sinai Desert and Palestine, active patrolling to gather information and harass the enemy, and flashpoints of action.

Once an adequate water supply was established at Romani, which did not happen until November 1916, the British forces felt themselves able to advance across the Sinai Desert. El Arish was taken on 21 December and Magdhaba two days later. Rafa, on the Egypt-Palestine border, was attacked in January 1917 with the NZMR Brigade carrying out a successful flanking manoeuvre that brought the brigade in on the enemy's rear. Rafa was taken, along with 1500 Turkish prisoners.

With the completion of a water pipeline and a railhead to Rafa, the Allied conquest of Palestine began. Gaza was the Allies' first objective and it was nearly taken in March after the Anzac Mounted Division completed a successful envelopment of the town. But with success in their grasp and the Turks preparing to evacuate, the British commander ordered the attack on Gaza halted and withdrew the force back to Rafa. It was a bitter disappointment for the Anzac Mounted troops.

The second attack on Gaza occurred in mid April 1917, but the Turks, under the able leadership of the German commander, Colonel Friedrich von Kressenstein, had strengthened the Gaza defences and were expecting the attack. It was a costly failure for the Allies, despite their using tanks and gas in this theatre of war for the first time. Their losses numbered 6500 and the disaster here led to a series of command changes. The British commander, Lieutenant General Sir Archibald Murray, was replaced by General Sir Edmund Allenby. Harry Chauvel was elevated to command what eventually became the Desert Mounted Corps, the first Australian officer to lead an army corps. Edward Chaytor was promoted to major general and took over the Anzac Mounted Division, the only New Zealander to command an Anzac force at this level.

Allenby was determined to break into Palestine and set about doing this by focusing on Beersheba, which was encircled by the Anzac

Mounteds and carried in a famous charge by the 4th Australian Light Horse. Fighting continued for another week before the Turkish frontier defences broke and the Turks withdrew.

After a dash across the coastal plains and holding Richon le Zion against fierce Turkish counterattacks, the New Zealanders galloped into Jaffa on 16 November. Jerusalem was taken on 11 December as 'a Christmas present to the British nation' to use the words of the British Prime Minister Lloyd George. It was a great morale boost in the hardest year of the war.

Jericho was the next objective set and it was taken on 21 February 1918, after a successful outflanking manouevre by the NZMR Brigade.

After garrisoning the unhealthy Jordan Valley through the discomforts of summer, the Anzac Mounteds took part in General Allenby's final offensive against the Turks and Germans in September 1918. The decisive attack was directed against Megiddo, while the Anzac Mounteds and attached troops carried out an important diversionary attack. Crossing the Jordan River on 22 September, they captured Amman and Es Salt, which had beaten off two earlier attempts to take them. More than 10,000 prisoners were taken at Amman.

The Turkish Army was now in full retreat and the Anzac Mounteds pursued them relentlessly, covering some 70 kilometres in five days. They were the first of Allenby's troops to enter Damascus on 1 October and pushed on northwards to Aleppo. With her army disintegrating, and her Central Power allies nearing collapse under the weight of continuing Allied offensives and blockades, Turkey requested an armistice, which came into effect on 31 October 1918.

At the end of the war the Mounted Rifles remained in Egypt as part of the garrison troops, where they helped suppress rioting in March 1919. A regiment was sent to Gallipoli to monitor the armistice. In June 1919 the NZMR Brigade sailed for home, leaving nearly 700 of their number buried beneath the soil of Egypt, Sinai and Palestine. They are scattered in war graves throughout the Middle East: at Gaza, Beersheba, Haifa, Damascus, Jerusalem and so on. A further 1200 Mounted Rifles had been wounded during the three years of campaigning.

While the Sinai-Palestine campaign had been tough going for the soldiers and easy or cheap victories proved nonexistent, it had ended in a decisive defeat for the Turks. It was a victory of strategic importance for the Allies, and the New Zealand and Australian soldiers fighting there had played a central role in achieving it.

There are 12 letters in this section. While they describe most of the key actions in which New Zealanders were involved, the letters also give the reader some understanding of what it was like to have to live and survive in this most inhospitable of places.

Bert Harris (pictured) wrote this letter to his mother early in the campaigning, immediately prior to the New Zealanders being sent to Romani. He was part of a machine gun squadron.

Somewhere in Egypt
10 March 1916

My Dear Mater

It is some time since I last wrote, with the exception of a service card sent a few days ago.

We have been on the move a good deal, which unsettles one for writing. We are still cursing the event tenor (I wish it was the Turks) of our way. It is quite an agreeable change riding about the countryside on horseback after being footies [infantry].

I am really stuck for something to write about and not sure what the censor will consider a fair thing. I have been over most of the country where the Turks made their futile advance on Egypt last year. Their route is marked by isolated graves and general debris left by a retiring force. We lose our horses once again, but are assured it is not for long. The weather is getting hotter, but is still quite bearable.

Just fancy, I have been twelve months in Egypt, or should I say it has been twelve months since I arrived in Egypt. Needless to say I do not look forward with any great pleasure to being in this sand-ridden country. It seems very much like it, though.

All our supplies are brought out to us on camels. They are indeed wonderful creatures. You can pack anything on them, from road metal to cans of water. The latter are square and weigh about 250 pounds. It is quite common to see great trains of camels numbering well over one hundred, all with great boxes full of rocks being carried out into the desert for roading.

How I wish J. Turk would come, it would break the monotony some.

It is close on a month since we have had mail, but we expect some any day now.

Strange, really, what an exhilarating effect mail days have on us. We all cheer up wonderfully for days after a mail, whereas now, having been without mail for so long, one gets quite irritable. The difference will be quite marked for a few days. See what good work you people the other end can do by writing regularly.

As is usual with the army one is called away at odd times on some duty or other. Such has been the case and I am starting on this some twenty-four hours later. We have been constantly on the move recently, but we are now digging ourselves in once again. We have been interrupted with a most violent sandstorm, the worst I have ever experienced.

Another full stop made to continue sapping. A party of seven of us are manning a machine gun in the trenches. We made a start this morning, making an empalement and building a mess room. We happened to have plenty of timber, matting and white duck canvas and as tuckering and living in the one 'bivvy' is conducive to the fly pest, we decided to have a good mess room. We have built a real corker. Of course, it is a good deal underground for obvious reasons, but you should see it. We have built a table and have a tablecloth of the afore-mentioned white duck. It seemed so strange sitting at a table again. Instead of laying about on the ground in hurriedly erected covers, we are sitting at the table, some, like myself, writing while others are playing cards. It is far too good to last. We have tried to make ourselves comfortable before, but no sooner had we done so than the order came to 'pack up'. When we did get orders to evacuate the 'Dards' we had just finished digging and finishing off a 'grand hole' in the side of a hill. We were quite prepared to stop there all winter.

The fates, or should I say the powers, (and quite rightly, too) ordained otherwise. There is really nothing very exciting about this life at present. I have seen a couple of snakes in their native element and helped to dispose of them with a waddy. I was riding out some few mornings ago to assist another section with a little trench work, when a fox was seen not a couple of hundred yards away. There were five of us; with a yell we gave chase. All were carrying something in connection with a machine gun. One had a two-gallon water can, another a flame extinguisher, a six-inch piece of piping, say, two foot six inch in length; in fact, we all had something too inconvenient to be packed. We did have a gallop through drift sand that threatened to throw our horses after coming suddenly off a hard patch, but needless to say the fox won. It was just playing with us. Cunning as a fox is an apt saying, I am quite convinced. He just ran along leisurely, but took fine care to keep a certain distance in front of us . . .

My word, I must say more about our mess room. We are a lot of youngsters with a new toy. You should have heard us today while building. One would suggest one way, then six others would all suggest something different. One was going to put a shelf in the corner, another would want to put up a hat rack here and so on. It is remarkable how energetic we all got and the vim with which we went about it. The life is monotonous, you know, and anything fresh sort of gives one some-thing to occupy one's mind.

It is going on for eight o'clock and one of the boys (a good mate of mine, name of Priest, has a place at Te Aroha) has been pottering about outside fixing steps so as we can climb down (not up), to our 'soup kitchen'. By force of habit, instead of sitting on the form around the table he throws himself on the floor, our usual resting place. I have many good cobbers here. One of them, sitting alongside me now, I must tell you of. He is a giant of twenty (weighs over fourteen stone) with a baby face, and the heartiest laugh I ever remember hearing. Most infectious. Such a dry old stick; we call him Tiny. (His proper name is Oldfield.) His movements resemble those of a baby elephant.

A more even-tempered fellow would be hard to meet. I could write you for hours on the different characters one meets in this outfit, but will desist as I do not think it would interest you. You meet all Dickens' characters here. Mark Tapleys, very seldom. Pecksmiths and Uriah Heaps, occasionally. Even Bill Sikes, unfortunately, are represented. The dude from Colleges turns out a cut, in fact, anything but the gentleman his education should have made him, while the farm hand,

and the hard case from town or country turns out the best soldier and mate. The man all gat and show proves often useless, while a quiet, unassuming fellow may have all the brains. This has been a great experience, and I must say an education for me. A lot of my pet notions have gone by the board. I consider myself a very smart fellow at times, but I have not such a high opinion of myself that I formerly held. One learns, eh? Nothing can be gained in this outfit except by a stroke of luck, but by paying strict attention to detail and learning your lot thoroughly.

Robert Tuke's letters to his sister Trixie describe some of the key events of the Sinai-Palestine campaign. In his letters are descriptions of the Battle of Romani, of the taking of Beersheeba, and of the New Zealanders' entry in to Jaffa, as depicted above. These letters are part of the manuscript and archives collection at the Alexander Turnbull Library, Wellington (MS Papers 1547).

7 August 1916

My Dear Trixie

We had a very exciting time during the last week. On Friday morning at 1 o'clock we all had to saddle up and stand to our horses. We had an idea the Turks were up to some mischief. At 2.30 a.m. they attacked our position on all sides. I don't think they knew that they had a good many thousands of men to deal with, including several brigades of Australians and New Zealanders.

German aeroplanes were very annoying because they were dropping several bombs among the troops and horses. I mean to say they tried to, but generally missed. It was not long before our troop leader, Lieutenant Ian Cruickshank, was hit in the back with a bullet.

We had several others wounded, but none in the Wellington Regiment were killed on Friday. We haven't heard yet what casualties Auckland and Canterbury had. The brigade they are in attacked the Turks from the other side. We captured several hundred Turks and I think altogether 4000 to 5000 were captured. Not bad, was it?

We followed them up on our horses on Thursday, but they made the chase too hot for us, so we had to return, but their positions were taken by Tommy Atikens later on . . .

The Turks are now about 12 miles from here. This Monday morning we had had two days' spell. Yesterday some of us had the beautiful job of burying dead Turks. Tonight at seven o'clock we are starting out again. I expect to follow the Turks. We are going to be out for three days at the least. We expect to have a pretty hot time of it. Our doctor and medical sergeant were both very badly wounded while dressing a wounded man. Our squadron leader was also hit. Captain Somerville is now officer commanding of our squadron.

Jack Stodart is in the hospital. A week ago he got a very bad kick just above his left knee from a horse. I expect he is in Port Said . . .

I will write again as soon as we come back, if everything goes well. Very best of love to you all.

Bob

Jaffa
22 November 1917

My Dear Trixie

At present I am on outpost a few miles north of Jaffa. I haven't written any letters since October 24, so I expect you will be interested in receiving some news . . .

Since October the 26th, the New Zealand Mounted Brigade have gone through several hard fights and the most interesting country since we left the Suez Canal zone. We have had some heavy casualties, but mostly wounded. We are quite certain that on our own front for every one of us hit, we killed around ten Turks, leave alone their wounded and prisoners. Our artillery is the stuff . . .

Beersheba is about 25 or 30 miles south of Gaza. Our Mounted Division had to assemble on the evening of October 30th and arrive . . . on the other side of Beersheba. We had a very long ride. We made a great success of things. When daylight came on the 31st we found ourselves in sight of Beersheba and some strong redoubts which we had taken. As per usual I was not hit, but my good horse was, but not severely. The Turks' heavy artillery got on to us. Our infantry were attacking Beersheeba on one side and our Mounted Division on the other. Beersheeba fell late in the afternoon. The next day the mounted men got well on Jacko's heels. Our regiment did well, we advanced from one ridge to another, capturing several prisoners and machine guns.

On the 31st and 1st November our troop had the misfortune to have nine of our horses hit. On the 1st a machine gun caught us.

On Sunday 4th we spent the day holding a ridge against the Turks, who made a strong show on the opposite side 1400 yards away. We went into action about nine in the morning. We left all our coats and warm gear on our horses. We were on the ridge all day and the Camel Corps were supposed to have relieved us that night, but they did not turn up. The result was that our regiment was on the ridge all night in our thin shirts and it was one of the coldest we have ever experienced. We did curse the Camel Corps. This fighting took place on the Hebron–Beersheba road, 12 miles from Hebron. The next Sunday we went back to Bersheeba and left for a place called Sharia, where there was a big battle the day before. We were then crossing from the right flank to the left flank, which is along the sea coast. On the 10th November, we had our biggest day's fight, just beyond a big village called Yebrak. The Turks counterattacked at about 4 o'clock and they ran into about seven or eight of our machine guns.

The Turks paid a big price for their stand at this place, which was their attempt to stop the New Zealand boys from taking Jaffa. The Wellington were the first to enter Jaffa on the 16th November . . .

No more news. Please let me know whether you receive this letter from Jaffa on pink paper.

Bob

※

This letter was written by Benjamin Marle to the parent of a deceased friend. Trooper William James Lunnon, 4th Troop, Auckland Mounted Rifles, was mortally wounded during a skirmish with the Turks five miles north of Jaffa. He died on 16 November 1917 and is buried at the Ramleh War Cemetery in Israel. He is one of nearly 700 New Zealand soldiers killed during the Sinai campaign. This letter is part of the collection of the Kippenberger Military Archive, Waiouru (2000.325).

4th AMRs
NZEF
29 November 1917

Dear Mr Lunnon

Having been Bill's pal for three years, I have to write and offer my deepest sympathy to you and yours in the sad loss of such a boy. The whole regiment, and especially our troop, miss his cheerfulness and for myself the whole outfit seems changed.

When we started off in the morning we had made up our minds we were to have more or less of a quiet day and the country and scenery were lovely. Before 10 a.m., however, we came in touch with the Turks, and you could hardly imagine a worse position, as wherever we went the Turks seemed to be able to enfilade us with machine gun fire.

It was easily the fiercest fighting we have seen and we didn't realise until afterwards that we were within 5 miles of Jaffa. At about 5 p.m. we were withdrawn from the left flank and had to reinforce the central position.

When we arrived on the scene we found Jacko had decided to make a charge and was under cover about 20 yards away. Our artillery had either finished their ammunition or else weren't advised of the position, so we had just to depend on rifle and machine gun fire. Jacko was shelling pretty heavily, and to make matters worse, Jacko himself started hurling hand grenades at us. From this position he couldn't raise sufficient courage to charge us and after pondering the matter a trifle too long he decided to run for it. It was then, when we jumped up to get into a better position for shooting, that the covering fire for their retreat got Billy. Although we were together when we started I somehow got in front of Billy and didn't know he was wounded for half an hour. However, some of the other boys saw him hit and dressed him immediately. Meanwhile, I was busy with an officer who was wounded by my side. The casualties were something awful and the most astounding thing is that any of us are left to tell the tale. When we got a view of the Turks retreating we fully realised what we had been up against. I don't think I am exaggerating a bit when I say there were eight Turks to every man of us and we learnt later that the brigade had put to rout a whole division of Turks which had been kept in reserve especially to harass our flank. From about 4 o'clock in the afternoon to 2 o'clock the next morning I was with Billy and he was fully conscious the whole time. He was shot through the abdomen and in cases of that nature they try to leave the patient as long as possible in the one position and so they wouldn't shift Billy before.

For about a couple of hours after he was wounded Billy was in great pain, but towards evening he seemed to brighten up a lot and the pain would only catch him periodically. When we put him into the sandcart he seemed quite himself again and he said, 'Well, Ben, I think I'll get over it now and I'll get a trip to England before I come back.' I myself fully believed he would recover, but it was evidently willed otherwise. When I heard four days later of his death I wouldn't believe it. One of the saddest sights was next day when we had to bury 20 boys of our own regiment and I thanked God Billy wasn't amongst them. So far I've been unable to find out anything about Billy after he left the firing line, as we advanced next day and after taking possession of Jaffa there was plenty to do. Until a few days ago we were not allowed to write, but now we have obtained our objective the mails have started again. We have been in two fights since the 14th when Billy was wounded and the regiment is now full of new faces.

Billy was by far the cleanest-living boy I know and was one of the few who haven't been spoiled in some way by being a soldier. He was always bright and cheerful and eager to lend a helping hand wherever he could and has been a true friend to me throughout. He was well liked by everyone who knew him and in expressing my own sympathy I know I am only echoing their sentiments.

As to Billy's belongings, all he had with him was in his wallets and these I have made into a small parcel and at first opportunity I will send it home. They were supposed to be handed into the orderly room and I did this at first, but we were continually on the move and so I got them back for fear they would be lost.

There are only a few curios and his shaving outfit. His watch, diary and photos, etc. were with him in his tunic pocket and should be forwarded to you from hospital. Bert Smith (a Bandsman) will probably have more of his things and they will be forwarded on. With the things I have in my possession is a money belt with £7 (three gold and four Egyptian notes) and a few odd collection coins. I'll send this along when I can post it myself.

Once again I offer our sympathy from this end. Billy did his duty well and faithfully and was better prepared to face his Maker than anyone I know in this outfit and we are all terribly sorry that such a one should be called to leave us.

God comfort you all in your sad bereavement.

Yours very sincerely,

Benjamin Marle

❧

George Ranstead (pictured opposite) sailed with the main body of the NZEF in October. A Gallipoli veteran, George Ranstead served with the Mounted Signal Troop throughout the Sinai-Palestine campaign. His service ended in June 1919 and he returned to New Zealand in October that year.

George Ranstead was a prolific letter writer, usually writing two letters a week to his parents, who lived at Matangi in the Waikato. These letters have been preserved and are one of the best records of the Sinai-Palestine

campaign. *Four folders of letters are housed in the Alexander Turnbull Library (MS papers 4139).*

A selection of letters are presented here. They cover a range of topics including the campaigns and the desert conditions. They also cover other diverse topics, such as the influenza pandemic of 1918–19, the use of aeroplanes in the campaign, New Zealand hospitals, the treatment of POWS and the New Zealand massacre of the men of Surafend village. George was sent to hospital in April 1917 after being kicked in the leg by a horse. He returned to his brigade late that same month.

Aotea New Zealand Convalescent Home
5 April 1917

Dear Mother and Father

I have not written lately as I have been waiting for news of the brigade and it has been a long time coming through. The casualties (Mounteds) so far as we have got them are very light — no Auckland officers and only a few men. I haven't heard from Tom lately, but I believe the brigade is more or less on the go the whole time and if so the post office won't be with them. My leg is just about better again. I was out yesterday for the first time but it is none the worse today — only a little stiff — like my luck. This is the first stunt I've missed and I'm getting back to the crowd as fast as I can.

The convalescent home here is the best in Egypt and quite a lot of officers grumble because they are not eligible for it. It is run by New Zealand sisters and a matron and is the nearest thing to a 'home' I've struck yet. They can't do enough for the boys . . . We have six meals a day (homemade scones and New Zealand butter for afternoon tea) and, really, if a man doesn't get fit here there is something vitally wrong with him . . .

I'm hoping to get out of here in the course of a few days, but will probably be held up at our training regiment at Moascar for some time. As a man leaves the brigade his place is filled up from the training regiment. So he is obliged to wait until another vacancy occurs before he can return.

Hope you are all well.

Your loving son,

George

Jaffa
Kaiserlich Deutsches
Postamt
19 November 1917

Dear Mother and Father

This is the first chance I've had of writing in the last month or so to tell you how things are going. Well, they're OK this end and I hope you are keeping well too. Am writing this in the German Consulate, where our signal office is established for the time being . . .

We have had a pretty eventful time since starting out on the stunt and I thought there would be heaps to write about, but I must be getting sleepy for I can't think of anything just now.

The evening I last wrote from (Beersheeba) we set out and travelled northwards for 30 hours going 'round and round the mulberry bush' sort of style and eventually fetching up at Askalon. From there we've moved about and fought a few times — camped at one or two Jewish villages where the people were very glad to see us, at length arrived at the above place, where the people aren't . . .

All along the line we passed ammunition limbers, spare equipment such as rifles, gas helmets, and bandoliers, and great dumps of ammunition from small arms size to howitzer shells and big plum pudding minewerfers. Gaza itself I haven't seen yet, but I believe it is just a mass of shell holes and the great redoubt of Ali Muntar is pretty well blown away. The place was subjected to a thorough bombardment from the sea and monitors played a big part in the shelling. The Beersheeba job was well carried out and everything went like clockwork. Our division carried out the encircling movement, travelling well to the south of the place and attacking from the east and northeast soon after daybreak. It was a long march of over thirty miles through country absolutely new, but we were in position and had our objectives taken before the infantry, who attacked from the west.

Enemy planes troubled us a bit during the first few days, but lately they haven't been so active. Ours were over in squadrons of twenty and thirty, and bombed everything they saw. They must have put the wind up the Turks to a great extent . . .

Will have to stop now as paper is short.

Your loving son.

George Ranstead

Jericho
3 October 1918

Dear Mother

. . . We have got as far as the above place after five days, but now it is a case of wait and see. There is no means of getting further forward just yet — all transport appears to be used for taking tucker forward and bringing prisoners back. I've never seen as many in my life before. All the way up from Kantara we were passing tramloads of them and Kantara itself seems to be crowded out. When the first batch landed there they marched them out into the desert and commenced to put barbed wire round them. They are arriving in this place in dribs and drabs all day long: Turks, Germans, Austrians, Armenians and Italians (escaped prisoners). It will take weeks to get them all into Egypt . . .

Our Brigade is about 40 miles away clearing things up and gathering recruits for the great Turkish advance on Cairo. Prisoners are coming in continuously and if a man falls out he is left on the road with a tin of water and told to come on to Jericho later. For miles around men are marching in quite unattended. I think they all know they are going to a good home. We told some German prisoners yesterday that Fritz had fallen, but they wouldn't believe us for a minute. One man who came from there said it would stand a six-month siege at least, and they absolutely laughed at the idea.

It speaks pretty well of our side to have taken the place so quickly.

Must stop now to catch the mail . . .

Your loving son

George

Richon
16 October 1918

Dear Father

. . . We are back out of the Jordan area at last and I hope we don't see it again. In the last move our troops operated to the east on Hedjaz railway, so you probably won't see much about it in the papers. They intercepted the force retreating from Inaar, about 100 miles to the south. Now we have been pulled out to refit, I suppose before moving on or away. Peace rumours are in the air anyway, as far as Turkey is concerned, I think they are pretty true . . . Heaps of fellows have gone away sick during the last few weeks — the climate Jericho way is about the most unhealthy we've struck yet . . . what do you think of the war now? Suppose you are picturing us all on our way back . . . not much news except that we're all a bit more cheerful than usual.

Your loving son,
George

In the field
11–18 November 1918

Dear Mother and Father

News came through this afternoon that an armistice with Germany had been arranged, which as far as we are concerned means peace. The news was received very quietly — somehow we have got so used to the present state of things that we scarcely realise it. I can imagine the people in England and France and perhaps New Zealand going wild with joy — strangely enough there is very little evidence of that here, but perhaps it will come later. I am waiting to hear what the conditions of the armistice are before doing any hand-clapping. They should be pretty good, though, as Foch has the arranging of them.

I received the news from division over the phone about three this afternoon. The operator who gave it to me said, 'Say, hostilities ceased with Germany at 0600 this morning — official news . . . take this S-M will you?' meaning carry on with the next message. Seems funny, doesn't it?

Later on the Indians to the north of us started sending up flares, hundreds of them, and the Jews all turned out to see the sight. When we told them the meaning of it they got quite excited, paraded all the schoolchildren and went marching up and down the street singing patriotic songs.

It is hard to say what will happen to us now. We may be about the front for months salvaging military stuff and patrolling the country. It is scarcely likely that we shall get away for some time, owing to the scarcity of shipping . . .

I won't be home for this Christmas, but next is a good bet.

Your loving son

George

*In the field
20 November 1918*

Dear Mother and Father
. . . On the 14th we went over to the scene of the Afur Khara fight and held a memorial service besides the graves of those who fell. It was the anniversary of the fight and the villagers turned out in full force. The graves had been done up beforehand by the schoolchildren here. They take a great interest in our crowd — look on us as their deliverers. It was in taking this place last year that so many casualties were incurred. The Turks counterattacked with a division of reserves and very nearly got us going, but were finally driven back.

Sergeant Kay of Te Awamutu was killed here. I am enclosing a photo showing a few graves — his amongst them . . .

Captain Allsop of Auckland, who was taken prisoner with eight men of Romani two years ago, is back again in the regiment. He is looking very thin and melancholy. The treatment they got was very bad. Indians were put over the white prisoners as NCOs. They gave our chaps a very bad spin in order to curry favour with the Turks. Allsop did seven months' solitary confinement for attempting to escape. Of the eight men taken with him five or six have died, so you can imagine what sort of time they had . . .

Love from

George

Richon
10 December 1918

Dear Mother and Father

. . . Last night a machine gun fellow was shot by an Arab whom he had caught in the act of stealing his kit bag. He chased the Arab and had got the better of him when the man drew a revolver and shot him at close range. He died in a few minutes. Our fellows are feeling very sore about it and want to go and clean the village up.

These things have been going on for a long time and as the culprits are very rarely caught it seems to us that the only way is to make an example of a lot of them. They are a bad lot anyway and only fear keeps them from being openly hostile. If they thought they could get away with it, they would do a man in for the sake of his boots. They haven't got any idea of humanity. When we were at Amman last March, there were hundreds of them hanging round waiting for a chance to loot our wounded or the Turkish — it made no difference to them . . . Up to now we have taken them pretty easily, but I can pick them getting a shake-up shortly.

Your loving son
George

Rafu
24 January 1919

Dear Father

Just received your letter of 29th November. Hope everyone has quite got over the flu by this time. I was surprised to see the extent it had reached, though by the cables we could see it was a serious out-break. Well, most of you seem to have had it and I'm waiting to hear that you are all better again. When you wrote that Bessie* was in hospital with pneumonia, that seems to be the thing which causes all the mischief . . .

Canterbury Regiment, which went to garrison the forts on the Dardenelles and also to fix up the graves of our men there, returned to

* Bessie later died as a result of contracting the flu.

the brigade yesterday. They had a pretty rough spin . . . The graves registration business was a bit of a failure. All the crosses had been removed, either for firewood or to make overhead covering in the trenches. Many of the graves were uncovered and the whole place was strewn with bones. They say the place represented a shambles, though I haven't spoken to any old hands yet. The new men were very impressed, but probably they hadn't realised the intensity of the fighting. Anyway, they do now.

Love for Mother and the family,

George

The Western Front:
France and Belgium
−1917−

T he year 1917 was, without doubt, the worst year of the war for the United Kingdom and the Dominions. For the United Kingdom, the massive losses of the failed offensives on the Western Front was compounded by the hardship of an island nation being driven to starvation by unrestricted submarine warfare. After three long years of attritional warfare and the end nowhere in sight, the warring nations were growing weary and nearing exhaustion.

For New Zealand, 1917 was a long, hard year — the only full year of service for the New Zealand Division on the Western Front. Brought up to full strength after their experience on the Somme and having spent considerable time in training the new arrivals, the New Zealanders undertook their first large offensive in the middle of the year. On the morning of 7 June 1917 the New Zealanders and Australians stormed the Messines Ridge in the Ypres Salient. Their job had been made much easier by the meticulous planning of General Sir Herbert Plumer and the Second Army Staff, planning that included the detonation of 19 huge mines beneath the German front-line trenches. The New Zealand attack at Messines was a great success, and apart from the attack on 4 October, it was the only success the New Zealanders were to experience in 1917.

The New Zealanders returned to the Ypres Salient in October to take part in two great attacks. The first, launched on 4 October 1917, was a stunning success and all the allocated objectives were easily taken. The next attack, made just over a week later, on 12 October, was a tragic failure and remains New Zealand's worst-ever military disaster. More New Zealanders were killed and maimed on this morning than on any other day since the European settlement of New Zealand. October 12, 1917 was indeed a black day for New Zealand as the long casualty lists and the letters here testify. In December came another failed attack at the Polderhoek Chateau by the 2nd New Zealand Infantry Brigade. This minor action, a costly failure for the two battalions involved, capped off a hard, difficult year for the New Zealanders.

These disasters were aggravated by the weather of 1917. With a late spring, no summer to speak of, the heaviest rainfall in 75 years and one of the worst winters on record, it was little wonder that morale in the New Zealand Division plummeted. The end of 1917 was truly 'a winter of discontent' and the spirit of the New Zealand Division reached the depths of despair. Other armies, the Russians and the French for example, mutinied or fell apart in 1917. It is a great tribute to the courage and tenacity of the soldiers of 1917 that there was never any danger of this occurring in the New Zealand Division. Still, every division has its breaking point and the New Zealanders in 1917 nearly reached the limits of their endurance.

The losses associated with the major actions of 1917 are very heavy indeed: 6500 at Messines, 7500 for the two actions at Passchendaele, followed by more than 3000 for the winter months of 1917–18. Every one of these was a person with a family, with friends, and with their hopes of a return to New Zealand and a better life there.

There are twenty letters featured in this section of the book. Some of them have been edited in order to concentrate on the essential information they contain and to avoid repetition. Three letters deal with the Messines attack, while five concentrate on life in the trenches in 1917. Ten letters cover the attacks at Passchendaele and one deals with conditions in the trenches after Passchendaele. The final letter in the section, written by Reginald Calvert, reminds us that, no matter how bleak the year of 1917, the New Zealand soldier never lost his sense of humour. In fact, a sense of humour, like mateship, national pride and self-respect, was one of the vital coping mechanisms that helped sustain New Zealand soldiers through the dreadful conditions of the worst year of the war. In 1917 these coping mechanisms were stretched to their limits.

⚹

Lawrence Sarten (pictured) was very fortunate to survive the war and return to New Zealand. Originally from Wanganui, Lance Corporal Sarten served as a Lewis gunner in the 3rd Battalion, Canterbury Infantry Battalion. He suffered 22 wounds in the course of the war, including on 4 October 1917 at Broodseinde.

France. Thursday
14 June 1917

I wrote last on 3rd June, and have received your letter of 8th April. On the 6th June, I received six altogether, yours of 8th April, Ruby's 1st April, Lily's 1st, 8th and 15th April, and Pearl's 15th April. Since leaving you I have received three parcels, Roy's fish and such, your cake and ginger nuts, and lollies and soap in two small packets from Pearl. We are resting now for a day or two, as we have just come out of the front-line trenches. We were working behind the trenches for a few days only, and the enemy's shells were dropping in the place where we were working, and also in our camp, but we had no mishaps. 37 days after Ruby's birthday (4th May), 10th June, we were taken into the trenches and the Company I am in was put in the very front line of trenches, only about 100 yards from the enemy's front line. That was my first experience of actual war, and I am just as pleased that we went to the front line for our baptism of fire.

96

We came out last night for a spell. On our way into the line a heavy bombardment was going on, and we were in the middle of it, so it took some time for us to get to our position, as there were a few casualties before we got in. The first day the enemy evidently expected an attack, and was continually shelling, and altogether there were three heavy bombardments on the first day. At the front nearly everything is done at night, when it is dark, so a vigilant watch is necessary, which is trying for the sentries. During the time we were in, I was always in the front line, and I have managed so far to survive it all. We caught it fairly hot though, and several times I was showered with dust, stones etc., which were thrown up by a big shell bursting quite close. One has to crouch down as low as possible, and trust to Providence, as there is no escape, and one may be hit by a shell any minute, as they burst all over our lines. The first day I was hit rather hard by a piece of hot shell (about the size of a finger) which struck me on the ankle, but apart from feeling sore for a minute or two, it did no damage, as it did not penetrate my boot. Our casualties were small, but it is hard to see one's mates being struck. Corporal Russell, who is in the platoon photo I sent you (in the sitting row next to the sergeant), was blown to pieces by a direct hit from a shell the first day. He is a cousin of Reg Collier, and used to work in Levin and Company's in our town.

You remember when you came down in the train with me before I left, there were two ladies who had a lot to say in the carriage, and had to travel 2nd class with 1st class tickets? Well, the boy who was with them, probably a son, who they were going to farewell, was killed. He was in our Company, and was in a dugout that was blown up by a shell. Andy Harrison got a bit of a slight smack on his hand, and the son of Gaze the grocer was also hit on the hand, both are from our town. One can do with very little of trench warfare, as it is really cruel, and one does not know when one's time will come, as casualties are announced by different men every few minutes.

One night I went with three others, and an officer and corporal, to take some bombs over no-man's-land into the enemy's front line, which some of our men had taken after the enemy evacuated to his second or third line. These are risky jobs, and one may be caught by machine-gun fire, which plays on no-man's-land (the ground between our front line and the enemy's) almost continually. These journeys are done at night, and the enemy sends over star shells, which light up the ground to enable them to see if we are coming over to attack them or make a raid. We get very tired and sleepy, as we are on duty day and night, and get sleep for an hour or so just when we can, and we always sleep in our clothes, boots and equipment in case of attack. Water is the great trouble, and one washes whenever one can save enough water. In wet weather it must be trying, as all we have is an oil sheet and a great-coat, and we sleep anywhere amongst the dirt, and we get annoyed by great rats, which are everywhere. One bit our corporal's ear when he was asleep. We are getting ample food, which is carted or carried some distance through the trenches, amid shell fire.

Keep a look at the papers at the doings of our men, as I will probably be in or near it. I was speaking to Max Smart, Laurie Loftus and Charley Morgan (Cock and Coy) and I heard that Harold Whetton (Charley Harris's mate) and Len Ahearn were killed. Jack Dennedy, who bached with me at the beach, I heard was on 10 days' leave in England. I have not seen or heard of Harry, Norman or Hubert yet, I do not know their companies etc. I was speaking to Harry Langridge. The field cards I sent to you, Coral, Lily and Aunt Lou, I wrote in the front-line trenches, when we had been in three days.

✂

Robert Carville Bett (pictured) joined up in December 1914 and served on Gallipoli. He returned to New Zealand in April 1916 but volunteered again for active service just two months later. On 15 June 1917 Bob Bett was mortally wounded at Messines, dying a week later. He was only 25 years of age and this is his last letter home. Following this are two letters sent to the Bett family informing them of Bob's death.

Right Here
Sunday
10 June 1917

Dear Everybody at Home

Here we are again, still cheerful and confident, and if anything cheeky now that I have got through what all papers call the greatest victory of the war. I can't help but think of you as you must at this time be reading the descriptions and accounts of what we did and the anxious moments you must have. I did intend sending a cable, but as we expect to be in it again in a few days I have changed my mind, as in spite of losses, reinforcements are coming, and things look that way again.

Now, of course, the thing uppermost in any mind is the battle, and I only wish I could have a quiet spot, plenty of time, a free hand and no censorship to describe the scene that Wednesday morning. It was a strange coincidence that one spot we had to take was known as Birthday Farm, and that I should be there on my birthday, one birthday of mine that I'll never forget. You have seen some illustrations in Dante's Inferno of 'Hell' — that gives but a poor impression of the scene. 'Hell let loose' when we hopped the bags at 3 a.m. that morning just before we attacked. Mines were exploded, nineteen along the front — earthquakes are nothing to the shake — a thousand tons of high explosive was under the mine nearest us. The glare, smoke and fumes from that were bad enough, but our barrage of bursting shells and the machine-gun fire were terrific. Add to that Fritz's reply, the dark misty morning, the noise, the flares — all shapes, colours and sizes — and star shells. It made a scene grand, brilliant, but grim and awful. We didn't get far before men began to fall, then we crossed the stream, up the hill into his first line, on to the second, over that to our objective, his third line, right on top of the hill and in the remains of the town of [censored].

I can't describe all the doings or incidents in those great hours, but you are a different being, fear seems to vanish once you are going on. It seems nothing to stop and bandage up your wounded mates, and help them back to a point of safety, a shell hole. You take no notice of men killed alongside of you, even when you get their blood spilt on you. Then the fighting itself seems so different to what you expect: we came up to Huns and it seemed quite natural to flop down and shoot. They didn't make much of a stand, their hands soon went up. Coming to a dugout it's easy to drop a bomb down and enquire if anybody's at home. The only thing that made me wild or gave me the desire to kill was when we got to the ruins of the town. Machine-gun fire was cutting our fellows out — and the Hun fires right to the last minute, then up goes his hands — it's then, when you see them coming towards you, hands up after they have taken their toll, and it's our turn, you have to decide, shall I kill. But when you see the poor, frightened devils, hate isn't in our hearts; the Britisher has too big a heart, and the Hun knows it. He soon saw the game was up, and out they came in hundreds, and it had its funny side, to watch the batches of grey-clad men go past us while we trudged on, just pointing to the way back for them to go. And they went some too, each man had his tucker too, they still believe we are starving. And the signs they made to us to encourage us to spare them, one patted his water bottle to me, as much as to say, something good here, but I took no notice, sent him on. Oh, there are dozens of incidents, many pitiful, but most make you believe the Hun isn't as bad as he is painted.

Monday

That's as far as I got yesterday, for tea was on then I went to a voluntary church service, and bunk at night. Today we have been kept busy, so this is the first chance I've had to carry on. I got a wire from Jakey tonight, asking if I was all right, so I have just sent off a reply, saying, Tip Top, and so I am cheerful and confident. Now let me see, to go on . . . All day long the battle went, driving the Hun back till the close of the day . . . That night we were digging, and shelling was heavy, particularly where we were on top of the hill. The Huns got ready for a counterattack, but our planes twigged him, and it was soon smashed up, and the next day we were down deep enough to give us shelter. But, oh, what a heartbreaking thing it is to have them blown in on you, half burying you, you are tired, oh so weary, thirsty, dead beat, and again you have to dig, dig, dig. That night the Hun made his big attempt to drive us back, and fierce the job was, and disastrous to him, but it meant the first quiet night, and we got some sleep. I have never known anything to equal the parched throats of ours, the dust, powder, phosphorous etc., our faces black as soot, with little rivers marked in where the sweat ran down, made us the roughest, queerest lot imaginable, but weren't we proud.

The next day was spent cleaning up, burying our dead, and the Huns', and less said about that the better. Somehow we get wrong ideas, we forget the Hun is human like us, has his home, his loved ones and sweethearts, and it was pathetic to look through the private belongings of the Huns we buried, and see his photos, and little Bible and treasures. Headquarters have got them now, and may his people get them, some day. Needless to say, I have got my collection and souvenirs, which I hope to get sent to you. Amongst them are some postcards, and a letter that wasn't opened, some books, two buttons of the Huns we fought, Saxons and Barvarians, a buckle, some coins and a comb, all of which I got in dugouts.

Now I could go on and on telling you of the terrible havoc wrought, how the ground is churned up, tell you something of his impregnable position, fortifications in concrete 5 feet thick — not only one, but dozens — of his comfortable quarters, and lots of things I noted, but like most things they will have to wait, for it's getting near bedtime, and I wanted to answer all your letters that came the night we went into it. I sent a field card to let you know I got them, and I carried them through the fight and have them here to answer, but am afraid I can't say much.

Pat, I must thank you for your cheery note and pass on to J.B's letter of 1st April telling of 'Bis' work, and his doings, also that my house in Fritz Street isn't sold. Well, Dad, you know what I said and I know it's all right, for it doesn't embarrass me, and there's plenty of time before I get back. Mother sent me cuttings of the coachbuilders conference and I see Mr Fuller represented you. Now, mother, your two of March 29th to April 1st, and April 4th to April 11th. I can't go and answer them in full for tomorrow we go into action again, so I must hustle up and write to Min, and also try and parcel up my souvenirs, but as I carried them through that last affair I'm reckoning confidently on taking them through part two. So later on, Mother dear, you will get your reply from the only boy you write to, who is thankful to God for protection, who feels that He controls our future more and more, that all rests with Him, and in Him I faithfully trust. So again I face it cheerfully and confident, and close this letter just wondering a wee bit what I'll have to say and where I'll say it next week. To all those I love at home.

Heaps, tons of love to you all.

From yours

Bob Bett

Somewhere in France
2 July 1917

Dear Mr Bett

I have much regret in having to write to you about Bob's death, but I knew you would like to know how he met his death.

Well, on the 14th of last month our Company had a special piece of work to do, and Bob was in charge of the section I was in. We arrived at our objective all right, but as soon as we started to dig in a machine gun got on to us, and wiped a good few of our members out.

Bob was about ten yards away from me, and I did not see him get hit, but after I got down a few feet, and had some cover, I went round to see how Bob was, but one of the chaps told me he was in a shell hole at the back, wounded. I then went out to see him, but he was very bad, and he told me the bullet went in his hip, and into the base of the stomach.

It was not until yesterday that I heard he had died from wounds on the 23rd, and I was very grieved, because Bob and I were great pals, although we had only known each other about four months, and we went through the attack before this together.

Well, Mr Bett, you have my deepest sympathy in the loss of your son, and if there is anything further you would like to know I shall be only too pleased to tell you, if it is in my power to do so. My address is the same as Bob's.

I remain,
Yours sincerely,
(27568 Private) *Dave McNab*

HE HAS GONE WEST

You know our way of saying of a chum, 'Poor old Bob has gone west'. Soldiers' jargon, but I like the expression. The full meaning came to me shortly after I heard about Bob. We had had a bad afternoon, though a lucky one. I had been detained at Battalion Headquarters and I was riding home alone. I had just got out of the dangerous zone and was riding along a ridge. Just behind me and alongside, our heavies were roaring out and I could hear the crash of the Hun shells coming in and occasionally the whine of a heavy going well back. In front I could see the country bathed in the golden light of the setting sun and away in the west was a beautiful sunset, with the spires of a town silhouetted against it like a golden city. It seemed such a desirable place and so fine a place to 'go west', away from the noise and din and strife, to 'go west' to the beautiful peace of the setting sun. It seemed to me then a beautiful sentiment and I thought of Bob 'going west'.

[soldier unknown]

⚜

Cyril Molloy, MC (pictured) served in the 1st Otago Infantry Battalion. Like many other New Zealand soldiers, Cyril Molloy was wounded at Messines but recovered in time to be committed to the Passchendaele attacks, where they became further casualties. In Cyril's case Passchendaele was the end for him. He was killed in action on 11 October 1917.

Walton-on-Thames
New Zealand General Hospital
20 June 1917

My dear Mother
　　Long 'ere this arrives you will have seen my name amongst the list of wounded. As soon as I got a chance I cabled you to let you know that it was nothing serious. I am tip-top now and am able to get out on the

river and enjoy myself. In fact, today I would have made a dash for London, but my field kit has not yet arrived from France and I don't want to go to the useless expenditure of buying any more clothes.

When I was first hit I thought I had got it pretty badly — naturally I suppose. However, an examination proved I was all right. I got a bit of shrapnel in the shoulder and the wound is almost healed now. I also got hit in the back of the head — the bit of shrapnel somehow dodged my steel hat. I have had my head X-rayed three times and there is nothing in it. Of course, I mean shrapnel. I got a small cut in my ear — all right now — and the drum of my ear was perforated by the concussion of the shell, but is rapidly healing. When I look round and see some of the injured I begin to realise how lucky I was. It was a great day and I would not have missed the experience for anything.

We went 'over the bags' at 3.10 a.m., the big mines just going up on our left — a wonderful sight. The earth shook as great volumes of flames leapt from the earth. However, our barrage began almost simultaneously, so we did not wait to see more of the spectacle. The chaps were over before the barrage started and kept well under it all the way. I was in command of the 4th Otago Company and our objective was the Hun front line and support trenches. We gained our objectives without a great deal of resistance, the Hun almost without exception surrendering everywhere. They came out of the dugouts with their hands up shouting 'Kamerad'. There was little fight left among them. We ran into a couple of machine guns here and there, which caused us a few casualties. However, we soon fixed them.

Their machine-gunners are good. They fire until they have no hope and then put their hands up. These fellows got no mercy. Further on than our objective the Hun resisted more strenuously, but our fellows swept on and gained every objective according to time and exactly as planned. The worst part of the business comes when the objective is gained and we have to dig in. However, we got to work in good style and, although the chaps were dog-tired, kept them going until we were finished.

This was the most anxious time as the Hun was going well by then and sending over a fair amount of stuff. My Company had a good deal of entrenching to do and we were just about completed before I got hit.

We got word that the Hun was massing for a counterattack from a certain direction and Brigade wanted new trenches dug to meet the case. I was just plotting it out on a map and getting the exact location of the trench when I got landed. Fritz was going solidly at that time. The 4th Division of the Australians were going through us. He spotted them and put over a high explosive shrapnel barrage, of which we got the benefit. However, he did not have nearly the concentration of guns we had and his stuff was not nearly as deadly. These shells were bursting all around us, but unless they came practically on top of one no very heavy casualties happened. He put over a fair amount of shell gas, which is a fearful nuisance. He put over a lot when we were on our way to the assembly trenches. It was very awkward, getting along the saps with a helmet on. To my mind we had only one man gassed.

However, the whole thing was a great success, but I am afraid the casualties are not light. We seem to have had a fearful lot of officers' casualties in our battalion. In my Company four of us went out. One was killed, two wounded and as far as I know the other man is still going. Anyway, Mother, we got off even more lightly than we expected. We have the Hun well beaten on land now, but they don't seem to know it — that is, the rank and file. I had about 11 hours of it — fairly strenuous going. In fact, as soon as I got out I fell asleep while getting moved down to the Casualty Clearing Station in a motor lorry. I walked from the line right down to where the ambulances were. The doctor wanted to send me in a stretcher, but I reckoned I could walk and stretchers were badly needed. I got down all right, the only thing that worried me was the thought that I might get another smack while I knew I had a 'Blighty'. A 'Blighty' means one that will take one to England.

I was hit on the 7th of June in the afternoon and was in a hospital at Calais until the 15th, when I came over here to Walton-on-Thames. I expect to go to Brockenhurst any day now, but I hope not yet awhile. I was supposed to go a few days ago, but am still here. I am enjoying myself immensely.

The only wound they worry about here, and which is nearly right, is the one in the head. My ear is getting right also. Consequently, I have been out boating on the Thames every day. Unfortunately, my tunic has not yet arrived or I would have gone to London today. I think I shall tomorrow if I can get away and borrow a tunic.

That is the difficulty here. All the fellows are without clothes and it takes a while to get them ones from France. When I finally get away from the hospitals, which I hope won't be too soon, I get a fortnight's leave and am immediately making tracks for Ireland. I shall write you a full account of all happenings.

Well, Mother, this is about all just now. I think I have enough money to see me round for a while, but could have saved more in France. I shall be more careful next time.

Hoping May and Ailie and Jim are tip-top;

Love to all,

from,

Cyril

∞

In this second letter of Lawrence Frederick Sarten, he describes what the trenches were like in June 1917. The above photo shows New Zealand soldiers in front-line trenches in the Somme, 1918.

France
15 June 1917

I wrote to you last on 25th May and have received your letters of 1st, 8th, 15th and 22nd April. We are resting after having experienced a term in the front-line trenches, where we remained all the time we were there. We have had a swim in a river, have been given a bath, and change of clean clothing. I have not seen Hubert, Norman or Harry yet, but Alf is with my lot. I was fortunate enough to escape being hit, but it is really a cruel business, and very trying and dangerous for all. There

106

are shells bursting everywhere, and one has only to keep low and trust to Providence, for one gets showered with debris from shells bursting a few yards off. It seems hard to hear of one's mates being killed or wounded. Gas is liable to visit us any minute, and a few of our men were caught.

I cannot write very often now, as we are always on the move, and it is most inconvenient making a start on a letter. The card I wrote you was written in the front line about 100 yards from Fritz's line. We are being well treated and have plenty of good, wholesome food. This seems a very nice country, and everything looks so green and beautiful at present. I am in want of nothing at all, and can easily get anything I want here. My health has been much better than I had ever hoped, so I am pleased about that. I had a letter from Jessie Guise and five others from the family (ours) today.

I met numbers of my old friends, including Reg Collier, who worked with me. I have had three parcels, one from Roy, one cake from Mother, and the soap and mixed lollies from you and Pearl. I am quite as contented as could be expected, so you must consider me to be quite all right until you hear otherwise. I thank you for the many letters you have sent me, which I have been thankful for. Kindest regards to Hubert.

Your loving brother.

Lawrence

※

There are two letters here from Gerald Noel Rudkin, both written to his sister, Gus. They describe life in the trenches in 1917. Unfortunately, Gerald did not get his leave to 'Blighty'. He is one of the 'missing' of Passchendaele. Gerald Rudkin was one of four brothers who went to the war; three (Gerald, Ernie and Edgar (pictured)) were killed and even the one who returned to New Zealand — Alf — did so in a severely wounded state.

In France
18 June 1917

Dear Gus

In answer to your letter dated April 22nd, yes I am glad that the winter is over, although it's too hot now, but you can't beat a soldier for growling. In fact, I won't be sorry when it's all over. We are having a bit of a lull at present, busy you know consolidating the ground that we gained last week and when that is finished I expect we will be on the move again. This old war of ours is getting harder every day — nothing but work. And I came here for a rest — not the long one you understand. Alf, I suppose, has written to you. He joined up in time for the push and came through it has far as I know. I have seen him once or twice since the stunt started, but have not seen him since the last time his battalion came out of the line, although his battalion is camped only a few chains down the road. I went down last night to try and find him, but it was like trying to find a needle in a haystack. In any case, they were going out on fatigue at 8 o'clock and us at 11 o'clock. All the work, you know, has to be done at night time. How sick I am of these long, silent, night parties (single file) stumbling and cussing in the dark. The one bright side is that we have got the wind well up Fritz (he gets it up us sometimes). He is leading a very unhappy life at present. I expect Ernie and Dora were excited when he drew the marble. I must write and tell him I am glad to hear that he is coming over. You get a lot of fun, even if you don't get much money. Well, Gus, I am writing against time so must say goodbye.

I remain
Your brother
G.R.

France
3 August 1917

Dear Gus

Just a few lines in answer to your letter. The weather is rotten at present, so I am not in writing form, it's also my birthday with no way of celebrating it, which doesn't help matters, however, it's wartime. I have got transferred into the same Company as Alf, so my address will be the same as his, with the exception of the number, of course. We have been doing a bit of training, but the weather has stopped that. I have been having instruction with the Lewis gun and am waiting for a fine day to go on to the range to finish up with it, but the way things look at present it will be our turn for the trenches before that comes around. My leave to Blighty is still a long way off. When the lists came out the other day I was fifty on it, which may mean months and may mean never.

Goodbye and for the present.

G. R.

✄

These are two of the last letters of Sergeant Harry Fulcher (pictured) of Auckland. Sergeant Fulcher was killed in action on 4 October 1917 during the first of the New Zealand attacks at Passchendaele. Sergeant Fulcher was a member of the Expeditionary Force to Samoa and a veteran of Gallipoli and the Somme.

NZEF
France
7 September 1917

Dear Mother

I am just scribbling you these few lines in answer to your letters, which I received a few days ago, just after I posted my letter to you. Those parcels you mentioned have not had time to get to New Zealand yet. It takes a long time for a parcel to go from here and I posted them in April and I hardly think they would catch that mail that was sunk — they were posted too early for that, anyhow. I hope not, because I put that old paybook in one parcel, also that shrapnel bullet from the peninsula. I had a German camera and a pair of field glasses, but they are both too heavy to register, so I took them over to England with me and left them with one of the sergeants of our Company. His people live just outside London and they promised to take care of them until I can get them back to New Zealand. I suppose you have heard about all the main body men going back for a six-month trip. The first batch will be leaving here very shortly. There are very few of them left now and they are going back at the rate of 250 per month, so it won't take long to work up to my turn. I'm classed as the 5th reinforcement just now. They made no provision for Samoans, but I heard that they were thinking of letting the Samoans away immediately after the main body, that is, if you have been in the forces all the time and have never been discharged, so I have great hopes of getting away from here before the winter is over. What a time I would have if I got back to old Auckland for two months. They guarantee two months' leave in New Zealand. I have a great friend of mine who is to go back with the first lot and I will send him up to see you. He is a real fine fellow and you will like him very much. He is an Auckland boy and was transferred into this Company at the same time as I was and we have been in the Company together all through. We are at present out for a spell and are having a great time of it. The weather is fairly good; we have an occasional wet day, but we can't expect anything else for the time of the year. The winter will soon be on us again now, only I hope I do not have to put in another winter here — last year was enough. How is Jack Bidwell getting on? Have you heard from him? I saw in the *NZEF Chronicle* that he had been wounded, but it did not say how he was getting on. I hope he gets on all right. He must have had a very bad shock, but I think he will get over it all right. It's very seldom a case like that is permanent. Young George Neal is just about due here. I have two cousins of his that live in Birkenhead in my platoon and they have told him to try and get into this Company, so he will most likely turn up one of these days. I had a letter from Nan last mail and I answered it yesterday; I also got those papers you sent. I like to get an *Auckland Star*, it always gives all the news of Auckland. Well, I think this is all the news just now. I will write again in a day or so. Give my love to Nan and Dad.

With best love to yourself
I remain
Your loving son
Harry

NZEF
France
14 September 1917

Dear Mother

Your two letters dated 10th and 18th July were to hand yesterday, so I thought I would answer them . . . while I have the time to spare. I was sorry to hear of that mail going down on the *Mongolia*. Most likely there was letter or two of mine on that boat, but I suppose it can't be helped. There are such a lot of boats sunk these days and I think the boats bound for the colonies have been very lucky so far. So Dad got that watch all right, and the other things. I did not post the registered parcel until a couple of weeks later, so you will have received it by now I hope. Thanks so much for those papers you have been sending. I received an *Auckland Star* a couple of days ago and after I have finished with it I will hand it over to some other Auckland boys who are in the Company. I was sorry to hear of Mrs Lindsay's brother being killed; she would feel it a good deal. I will be on the lookout for that parcel you posted. It will not arrive here for a couple of weeks yet. I have not received any letters from Mollie yet. I think her letter must have been submarined. I had a letter from Auntie Annie, also one from Maud. It is the first letter I have had from her for a long time and it is quite a time since I had a letter from Auntie Annie. She has sent me a parcel and it ought to arrive here very soon now. We are having a pretty fair time of it just now. We were reviewed today by Sir Douglas Haig. This is the second time we have been reviewed by him since we have been in France. We are camped at present quite close to Boulogne and I had a pass and went in there the other day to have a look round, but there is nothing to see after being over in England. Grannie wrote to me the day before yesterday and everybody is well over there. She was just going to write to Aunt Patience. I believe she had been inquiring how I have been getting on. Stanley Watson is looking well. I saw him yester-day. They are billeted some distance from us. Well, I think this is about all just now as it is getting late. Give my best regards to Mr and Mrs Morrison, also to Mrs McVea. I suppose Jimmie will be going into camp soon. Tell Maud Stewart I will answer her letter in a day or two. With best love to Dad, Nan, Eva and yourself.

I remain

Your loving son

Harry

❀

Lawrence Frederick Sarten's first letter covered the attack at Messines. This letter deals with the 4 October attack at Passchendaele, known as the Battle of Broodseinde. While the 4 October attack was a stunning success, it was still very costly in terms of its New Zealand casualties. Members of the New Zealand ambulance corps (above) were part of a medical team that worked in challenging conditions to save the lives of injured soldiers.

France
10 October 1917

Dear Mother

Just fancy, it is my birthday, but you would not know that I am in hospital seriously wounded. I was hit on 4th October during a big advance and we had gained our final objective at 9.30 a.m. I was digging in to consolidate our new front line when, at 10.30 a.m., a high explosive shell burst almost in my face. The boy digging a foot or two off me was blown to pieces and I was knocked down with the thought that my time had come. I soon came to and was being bandaged by my mates. I lay where I fell for 25 hours with some of my wounds undressed. The stretcher-bearers could not come up till then, owing to the heavy fire and the distance we had advanced. I was carried out (after lying in a wet, muddy shell hole — light rain falling almost continuously). I had to be carried on stretchers for about four miles and was put on a train, arriving here on Saturday night (6th) after receiving attention at various stations on the way. On Sunday I was operated on and again yesterday. My wounds are many: a full unexploded British cartridge (case and lead) was driven right into my jaw, and could not be seen. A bullet (lead part only) went in my left elbow. Something went right through my left foot — in at the front left side and out at the heel. About half a brass cartridge case went into my thigh, and about five other small pieces of lead, about this size, $\bigcirc$ went into my legs. So I have wounds in the face (one), left arm (one), right arm (flesh wound, one), right leg (full length, about five) and left leg (full length, about five) and left foot, a hole right through. Everything has been removed and consequently some gaping wounds are left, as they had to search for lead, etc. The force of the explosion must have driven the bullets (which must have been in my pouches, or lying about) into me. Most luckily I was not hit in the chest or body, my gear and gas helmet saving me. I was conscious for all the time, except the few seconds after I was hit. I am keeping all the bullets, so I will send them to you some day. I will probably be sent to England when it is safe to move me. It is very painful being dressed (the wounds) but it will all be right in time. I am getting on grand and it will be a long time before I have to join up again, so I will have the winter in England. I was in charge of a Lewis gun team in the advance and am wearing one stripe (lance corporal). An old Wanganui resident (some relation of Archdeacon Thorpe — from Putiki or up-river) called to see me, as I was from New Zealand. She gave me a handkerchief, writing paper and books. She said she would write to you. I seem the only New Zealander in this ward and am called the New Zealander. A Scotty gave me a nice box of chocolates today. You will know I am wounded before you get this and will be seeing the hospital reports. How I wish I could have your tender hands to dress my wounds and ease my position, but you can do nothing. I could not get better treatment here, I'm sure. They are so good and gentle. I will not write very often as I am not feeling too good yet, and have been sick today. Thanking God for my marvellous escape, accept my love.

Your loving son, *Lawrence*

⚔

Harry Gibbens (pictured), known as Cocky Gibbons, survived the horrors of Passchendaele and the war. He was a stockdrover on the West Coast and lived most of his life in Greymouth. He died in Auckland around 1957. While Cocky Gibbens' letter is hard to follow because of its more colloquial nature, its account of the fate of POWs and how the soldiers regarded the enemy is open and honest.

Codford St Mary's Wilts
25 March 1918

Dear [*Bill*]

Just a few lines to let you know I have not forgotten you all together. Well, Harry, poor Harry did not reign long over here at Ypres. Now, Bill, it was a trap for all of us. The bloody heads ought to have been sent over the top themselves instead of us. They had nothing ready and you were up to your hips in mud and water. I saw Harry that

114

morning and was talking to him. He went to the left of me, towards the Jocks. He was killed near the cemetery and Colonel Evans was not far away from him. I think the same bastard got the both of them. They were making for a gap in the wire at the time. We went there just after, but we had to get down and go to the right to get through, for he had a machine gun trained all along there. I went back that night to bury Harry and get anything he had to send it to you, but he was not there. I think he was buried with Evans, for they were close to one another. We went back that night. I could not find either of them. You can rest that he was buried, Harry, for sure. Not like thousands over here — left where they fell. Well, Bill, I have got another pack and rifle so I will be going overseas any time now. We have got word to hold ourselves in readiness, so that is enough for us to know. Well, Bill, I will have no mercy on any bastard, wounded or not, for they have none for us. We had two hundred prisoners in on 12 of October and a Jock sergeant came along and wanted to know what we were going to do with them. We told him the officer left us to mind them until he came back, so Jock minded them — all but about thirty — he bombed hell out of them. Jock has no mercy for the Hun. Jerry calls them the women from hell. Jerry has started with this push — all right so far — it is young. Yet . . . if he gets through with his calvary he has to pass the Indian Calvary and the Lancers and they are handy behind the line waiting for him. They are not bad, either. They take great pride in their horses — they say he is my best friend. There was a big draft of Australians and Canadians and New Zealanders and Africans and Tommies artillery that went away the night before last at midnight so as nobody would know they're moving about. I was on guard that night, so I had to let them through the gate and was told today nothing about it. When you get this it will not matter, for they will be well into it. They took 100 hundred [sic] guns with them on the train. They had them covered over with wire netting and hay and grass so the planes can't tell what they are. Well, Bill, [name deleted] is over here. I think he will be going home again soon. He has been turned down — he is a big cow-hearted bugger. He has got the wind up properly and is as frightened as hell. Well, Bill, I have no more news to tell you just now, so goodbye and be good. Remember me to . . . the girls and old Charley Moss.

    I remain yours truly friend

H Gibbens

My address is Rifleman H I Gibben 37033. 4 Battalion D Company France.

If you want to know anything write and tell me. If I can find out for you I will do it with pleasure.

We are going to the Somme as far as we know. So we are in for a hard time of it, for sure. Never mind, better luck next time.

✄

George Tierney (pictured) was a private in the Medical Corps at Passchendaele where he received an almost fatal dose of mustard gas. While the letter is unfinished, George did return to New Zealand, but remained affected by the gas for the rest of his life. This letter is important for two reasons. It shows the effects of gas on soldiers and the treatment of gas patients. Equally important, it shows the tremendous dedication of the New Zealand nurses for 'their boys'.

London
28 November 1917

My Dear Mother and Father
Before making a start, let me explain the reason why I haven't written to you before this, probably a reason which you have guessed at. One of the effects of the gas is to make one blind, luckily for the time being only, and for some time afterwards reading and writing becomes an impossibility owing to the eyes being in a weak state. This letter will have to be written in stages as my eyes are not normal yet.

I sincerely hope you have received the various letters written for me by various people. You will have received one such letter from a New Zealand nursing sister by the name of Reidy, a great friend of the Sisters Campbell; Mum and Dad, value that letter from Sister Reidy, for reasons which I'll explain later on in this letter.

You will have both read of the intense fighting there was in front of Ypres and more especially on the ridge known as the Passchendaele ridge. From a few days after the Messines battle (June 7th) the new

116

brigade of which I was a part was given the task of holding an important and warm sector between Messines in the north and Armentières further south (you can trace it on the map). The sector was known as the Ploogsteert sector. We were there for four months and I managed to get through all right. About September 12th we moved out from our headquarters (near Armentières) and by various means proceeded a distance of about 40 to 50 miles back from the line. The place was a quiet country district about 10 miles from the seaport of Boulogne. Of course, when I said 'we' I meant the whole New Zealand division. For three weeks we drilled and trained and most of us were as well as could be wished. At the end of that period we slung up our packs and for four and a half days trekked back to the line in the direction of Ypres. Eventually we arrived at a place called Poperinge; we slept in tents, with Fritz dropping bombs from 9 p.m. to 2 a.m. He must have dropped between two and three hundred bombs that night. A few of the New Zealand boys were hit.

There had been heavy fighting in the sector which we knew we were intended for and knew what to expect.

At last we proceeded up amongst the scenes of desolation and were posted to various positions in the rear of the line, ready for the inevitable rush of wounded. Along with others I was allocated to one of the pillboxes which had been captured from the Fritz during the recent fighting. Four of us were the last to arrive and all the room inside the pillbox was full up. The only remaining thing was to try and make a dugout in the earth. Rather a difficult job as (I say this seriously) every inch of the ground was a shell hole. We picked out the most suitable position and slaved away for hours until we had a passable shelter, *viz*, a hole into which we could just scramble. Night was approaching and we had taken down several cases. The last case before we retired for a rest was a man who had been buried in his dugout by a shell. The unfortunate chap died at our dressing station. I don't know how long we had been in our hole and in spite of the intense shelling I had gone to sleep. I awoke with the side of our dugout trying to crush me. It was an unpleasant sensation, but with the aid of a couple of cobbers I managed to get out with nothing more than a couple of scratches on my face. A shell had landed at the bottom of the side of our 'bivvy'. It was a strange thing, but I didn't hear that shell go off. After that I went and slept with the doctor. The above incident happened at 10 p.m., the boys were to 'go over' at 6 a.m. the following morning. Before going any further I would like to give you my impression of the British artillery barrage. It was grand, splendid, awful. Impossible to hear oneself speak. The big guns were about 2 miles behind us. Just imagine a circle as from Petone to past Day's Bay. Without exaggerating, for hours it was a continuous ring of flame. Just behind us were the 18-pounders and they are the ones to make the row. At 5 p.m. the artillery opened out with increased intensity and at the appointed hour our boys, along with four other divisions, 'hopped over'. All went well and everything planned was captured. I remember my feelings when just after the start of affairs I saw a string of about 250 Huns coming over the rise, without even a single escort. Some of our boys were just starting with a case and immediately four Germans detached themselves from the rest and gave our boys a lift. Honestly, the vast majority were delighted to be captured. Our casualties were usual with a 'stunt'. We were busy all day carrying out, and in the afternoon we moved up to a new position on the ground captured by our men that morning. Then the real hard work began. The ground was little better than a swamp and, of course, one mass of shell holes. We now had a distance of 2 miles to carry and believe me it was hard work; often we would sink up to our hips and under such circumstances could carry but a few yards without a rest. This continued for the afternoon, when we began to get the place clear. The 'place' was another pillbox, the range of which Fritz had to an inch. He had already killed a padre and four wounded that afternoon outside the door. We were ordered to stay the night in this pillbox (named Otter Farm) in case there were any more cases coming in. It is a strange sensation, being in an artillery target; at frequent intervals during the night he opened up on us with big stuff, but only hit the show once. For a roof the place had 9 feet of concrete, so you may rest assured that one hit didn't worry us.

After being there in the line for a week we were taken out and marched to a quiet place where we had another five days' rest. We learned that we had to go up for another stunt, in the same place. At the end of the five days we set out on the road once again and after a time we reached an old mill, which was to be our headquarters, where the colonel stays. It was situated about 8 miles from the line, and was used as a clearing station for walking wounded. In the afternoon of the 11th October a large military wagon pulled up and we were all bundled in. I can remember how happy we were, joking all the time, and a lot of the boys were never to see their homes again, for our field ambulance suffered the heaviest casualties ever experienced by a New Zealand Field Ambulance. The wagon took us as far as possible, when we had to get out and walk.

About 15 of us were detailed to bring up the rations. By the time we started out with the cases of food on stretchers it was dark and furthermore we didn't know exactly where we had to go. You have heard of Menin Road; well, we had to follow the remains of that road to get to our destination. The cases we had were very heavy and under ordinary circumstances would have entailed hard work, but to make matters worse the road was in the usual muddy state, we were up to the knees at every step. We wandered around and toiled through the mud for an hour, when we came to a part of the road where there was a block in the traffic. A horse wagon had got stuck in the mud and two tractors had got so far and couldn't move and the road was in such a state that the sergeant in charge of our party decided to leave the rations on the side of the road for the night. After some hours we arrived at our pillbox absolutely dog-tired. All the inside was full of artillery men, so we tried to sleep in the mud at the back of the pillbox. Fritz was landing them pretty close, but nobody was hit.

Still later on he put a barrage of gas shells about a quarter of a mile behind us. We all put on our masks and some kept them on for an hour. I kept mine on a little longer, and took it off. A little while after we were able to get inside the pillbox, owing to the artillery chaps having to go to their guns. There were two compartments in the place, shaped as in the following little diagram. Of course, you realise that the doors were facing the wrong way and it was quite possible for a shell to come right in the door, as we realised to our cost.

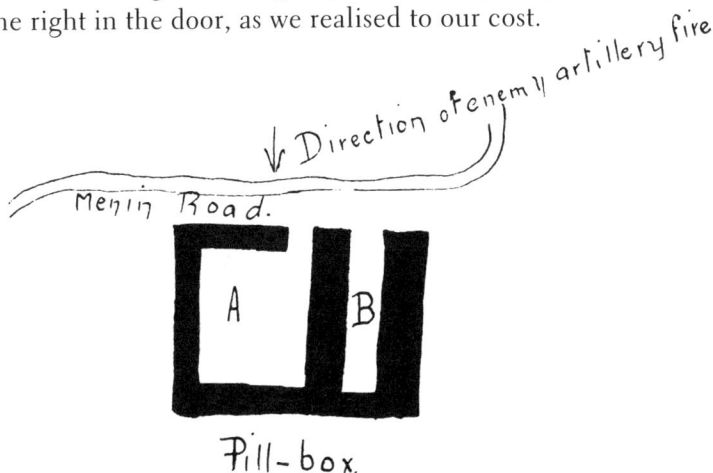

A and B are the compartments I spoke of. You will see that 'B' does not offer any shelter from a shell landing at the door. Three of our boys were in there, a shell landed at the door killing them outright. I was lucky and happened to be in compartment 'A'. About 8 a.m. the first stretcher case came down and our squad of six men were detailed to take him down. He was about 15 stone in weight and owing to the bad state of the roads progress was very slow and it took us about three hours to do a mile. Eventually we reached the end of our relay and the corporal in charge of our squad began to be sick and went to report to the doctor. I was feeling sick myself, so thought I would have a rest before going back. After I had been resting a while I began to vomit, and came to the conclusion that I had a slight dose of gas. I went to the nearest doctor, who sent me down to the field ambulance for walking cases. At this stage I was vomiting about every 20 minutes and felt a bit weak on it, but nevertheless I decided to walk down, although I should have been a stretcher case, but when you have been having guns banging in your ears for hours, the one desire is to get out of it. The man who walked down with me had his arm blown off, but nevertheless he managed to get down unaided.

After the first few spasms my vomiting changed to retching as I had had practically no food and my stomach was empty. Eventually I reached the roads where the traffic was running and managed to get a ride on an ammunition wagon, with the result that after some hours from my original starting out I arrived back at the place where our colonel and the remainder of our boys were running a clearing station for walking wounded. There was a chap in the Army Service Corps attached to our ambulance, whom I had nursed twice. Once on the boat coming over and again in England, with the result that he had a lot of time for me and looked after me just as my father would. After I had my particulars, etc, fixed up, this chap (Barclay was his name) took charge of me and put me into his bed, arranged something in case I was sick, and brought me hot tea. I had a lovely sleep and when I awoke the effect on the stomach had ceased and had seemingly transferred all its attentions to my eyes. They were all swollen and full of water and it was difficult for me to keep them open. At this stage (the evening of the same day) I was sent further back to an Australian clearing station. I was totally blind by 7 p.m. that evening and my eyes were constantly being bathed. They put a bandage round my eyes, and the agony was awful (this between you and I) — it was as though my eyes were full of sand.

Some were singing out, but I just kept my counsel and resolved to say nothing. After 36 hours I was placed in a hospital train, but immediately went to sleep and the next thing I remember is being placed in an ambulance at the journey's end. The place was St Omer, a town some 40-odd miles from the line. The ambulance visited several hospitals, but they were all full up. How lucky I was that they couldn't take me, for it might even have meant my life had I got in there, for reasons I'll explain. They were that busy that no case could have special attention. At any rate, I was taken in at No. 7 General Hospital and was put into bed in a tent. A sister came and had a look at me and seeing by my card that I was from New Zealand told me she was a New Zealand sister. What a lucky coincidence. I managed to ask her name and found it was Sister Drummond, a sister I used to work with at Trentham. I was in such a state that she couldn't recognise me, but I felt glad I was in her hands as she was famous for her devotion to the patients. I began to realize at this stage that I was dangerously ill, but all the way through I felt perfectly confident that I'd pull through all right. I got on the broad of my back and resolved to 'give it a go'. There were all gas cases in my tent and five died in two nights. A chap from our ambulance died next to me and I didn't know.

I subsequently learned from the sister that I was black for two days and she had doubts as to my recovery during those days. Of course, the danger lay in my lungs. Dear Mum and Dad. Of course, I cannot say for sure, but I reckon that Sister Drummond saved my life; she was the essence of attention and constantly kept her eye on me. As far as I know there are two dangers to be guarded against in cases of this sort. Heart failure and suffocation. Luckily I wasn't unconscious long and I kept all my facilities in detecting any signs of suffocation in myself. I only had to raise my finger and they had the oxygen on me. I was having champagne and brandy alternately every two hours, also some stuff given with the needle every four hours, all, I take it, as a stimulant for the heart. I was in the dangerous stage for a week when I was transferred to another ward in a large monastery. My luck was still in and I struck another New Zealand sister — Sister Reidy. I was still in a serious condition and a screen covering all but one side of the bed was erected and a steam kettle installed. I held my own for about a fortnight, not much better, but no worse, until one evening I seemed to get ever so much better all at once. I didn't use to care about talking, but on this occasion (about 6 p.m.) I felt quite chirpy. From then on I began to get gradually stronger, and cheekier, not insolent, but in fun. That Sister Reidy was good to me. Out of her own pocket she used to buy me eggs at 5d each, fruit and anything she thought I required. She is a big woman and it used to remind me of the mother of chicks, the way she used to look after the few New Zealand boys she had in the ward. Let anybody say anything to us boys and she was down on them like a ton of bricks. She didn't care a hang for colonels or anybody, and besides, knew her work from A to Z. Yellow Three Castles cigarettes and Havelock tobacco cannot be had anywhere here and she used to get boxes of both from New Zealand and distribute them among her New Zealand boys. Sister Drummond and her used to get their half day off together and spend it going round the various hospitals in St Omer, looking for New Zealanders, and seeing if they wanted anything, which they would provide somehow.

I spent three happy weeks in this ward and at the end of that period I was taken off the serious list, and I am told that a cable to that effect was sent to you.

On the 11th November (just about a year since I said goodbye to you at Wellington) I left St Omer for England. While I was waiting for the ambulances to show up I saw an artillery officer (New Zealander) make for a door. I thought I recognised him, so I gave him a call. He turned back and sure enough it turned out to be Miss Munro's brother-in-law, who I had often met at Janet's place. Wasn't it strange that I had been keeping a look out for him for months, and to suddenly meet him in such an unlikely place? He was quite good to me and we had quite a chat.

After a 56-hour journey I found myself at 10 p.m. in a large hospital in the East End of London. I was very disappointed that I didn't get to one of our own hospitals, but unfortunately our institutions were full to overflowing. I didn't like this hospital or its staff a bit, and the doctor, who had recently come from the States, knew absolutely nothing about my particular complaint. That's written soberly, for he asked me a lot of questions which any doctor with a knowledge of gas would have known himself. While I was in receipt of four medicines in France, here I got none. I was here about a week, when I was told I might get up. I had been up two days and had had five and a half weeks in bed when this Yank recommended me for discharge. According to custom, I went before the colonel, who had been a London specialist. He never even examined me, just looked at me and sent me back to the ward as certainly not fit to go out. The doctor got quite a shock to hear the result.

About July you posted me two very acceptable parcels. They reached my unit on 16th October, but of course I was away and in hospital. They subsequently reached me here in London on 28th November, along with the one sent by Gladys Anderson. A week or so later your parcel (containing cake) also arrived and, Mum and Dad, the contents could not have suited me better had I gone to a shop and ordered them. Especially welcome was the sugar and cocoa. Sugar is practically unobtainable here, also tea.

✄

Letters of Lance Corporal Robert Newton Hawthorne (pictured). Lance Corporal Hawthorne came through the Battles of Messines and Passchendaele unscathed. He died of wounds on 21 December 1917, just one month short of his twentieth birthday. A photograph of the boy soldier has been displayed in the family home ever since. It is impossible to be unmoved by the two letters sent to the family informing them of Bob's death.

France
4 August 1917

My Dearest Sister
Just a few lines in answer to your last welcome letter, which I received yesterday. I had a big mail the day before I came out of the trenches, but I didn't get yours till yesterday. I had eleven letters all

123

told, so what a contract I will have answering all that correspondence, however I must do so, as I can't expect letters if I don't answer them. I had a big letter from Mrs Hutchison, she is sending me a big cake, so there will be something doing when it comes my way; her two eldest boys are going into camp, one enlisted, and the following day the other one was called up, so she will be left in an awkward position as she is shifting down to the farm at Georgetown. She said she would have a good place for me to come to see her when I get back. Aunt Lizzie sent me a tin of chocolate and a tin of tobacco. The old pipe gets the devil now, as New Zealand tobacco is a very nice smoke. It was very kind and thoughtful of her to send me such sensible things. Well, old dear, this war is getting worse, the weather here is awful, the trenches are a regular bog hole, a fellow is wet from one weekend to the other, sleeping, or trying to sleep in wet clothes, that is war for you. You should have seen some of the other brigades who took part in the big advance, their clothes, what was left of them, were one mass of mud and slime. There has been a terrible loss of life and this weather has stopped us from pushing further on, so things are just middling. I was surprised at the German prisoners who passed me the other day — young boys, some of them about fifteen — they looked like a mob of pigs instead of human beings. Well, Myrtle, I have had the satisfaction of getting at close quarters with Fritz. I was on patrol every night with our team of machine gunners, and went out into no-man's-land near the enemy lines. We had several hot fights in the dark, our hand bombs and bayonets were very handy. Although they were always three to our one in numbers, Fritz was smacked up every time and left a heap of dead behind. The Lewis gun is a deadly weapon, as he has found out to his sorrow. One of my best cobbers was shot clean through the head. I miss him a lot, but that is a common thing here now, a man is soon forgotten. Well, dear sister, we all hope that this will be the final clutter and that Fritz gets licked, although a lot of the boys will be laid low over it. I haven't seen Sid lately, he is up in the line, I think. Now, Myrtle, I think I will have to make this do for the present, so I will now say goodbye, with best love to all at home. Give my love to Sibly, and heaps of love and kisses to yourself, from your loving brother,

Bob

France
18 August 1917

My Dear Sister

Just a few lines in answer to your very welcome letters, which I received yesterday. I received two of your letters together, so this one letter will equal them for an answer. I am glad to hear you are all well, but I suppose you will feel the cold this winter, after so much rain. I had two letters from Mary also, she said the *Waitemata* had arrived back to New Zealand safely and that Jim had gone to see her. I gave him two photos of Dad and myself to take back for me, as it was useless carrying them round. I find enough rubbish as it is. Well, Myrtle, the weather is getting cold again; we haven't had so much rain lately, but the mud is still plentiful in the trenches. The war is still raging fierce, you will see by the papers that the British have been pushing on; some say we are winning the war [censored] Our poor old Company has had a hard hit lately, it's a devil losing some of your best cobbers, but we can't all escape, some have to go under. The old soldiers often said that our Company was one of the unluckiest going, and so far they are not far wrong, but there is no use frightening you. I feel quite at ease about it, ready to take my chances with the rest . . . From your loving brother,

Bob

France
28 October 1917

My Dearest Sister

Once again I have the long-looked for opportunity of writing to you. Well, dear, I received your very healthy parcel, which just arrived at the right time, along with one from Maggie. I had just come out of the line after a severe time at the well-known hot-shop Ypres, and settled down in a nice quiet spot, so what a treat I did have for a few days. Everyone said you were a darling, and wished they had a sister who could bake like that. I also received a parcel from Mary while I was up the line, it was real decent of her, but I was so miserable that I couldn't do justice to it. Well, Myrtle, this war is getting a real devil. I see by today's paper that the Germans made a mess of the Italians, but the British and French are still pushing on. Our brigade made a name

125

for itself, we made a big successful advance against the Huns, took some thousands prisoners and made a general mix up amongst them. I was one of the lucky ones to get out alive. We had a good many casualties in the battalion, but our old 12th Company was very lucky. We had a couple of days out and then had to go back in again for close on a fortnight, and I can tell you it was worse on us than when we went over the top. Two of the other New Zealand brigades tried to advance about a week after us, but failed and were smashed up very bad. I have been wondering how old Sid got on. His Company were dished up very sore, but I hope he is alive. He may be wounded in Blighty, if he is he is damn lucky, out of it for the winter. Well, dear sister, I hope you have a good Christmas. I can't see myself having a good one, but never mind. I hope to some day. I must now say goodbye. With best love from your own loving brother,

Bob

France
26 December 1917

Dear Sam

Just a line to give you some of the news of your son, Bob, when he was wounded. It happened about four o'clock in the afternoon. I was stretcher-bearer and the word came along the trench to me. As soon as I heard it was Bob I got along as hard as I could and there was Bob lying in his dugout, hit rather badly, twice in each leg above the knee and twice in the right arm, once above and once below the elbow. I set to work at once, and bandaged him up and got him out of it. His left leg was broken, and rather badly hit, but I don't think he will lose it. We had rather a hard job getting the stretcher down the trench and they would only send two with it, but when I got about a quarter of a mile I met another company of men and I asked the captain for the loan of a couple of men to give me a hand, and he gave them. I wanted to get Bob down to the doctor as quick as possible. We had about a mile and a half to carry him. It was well after dark when we got there, and it was cold, and freezing very hard.

I was very sorry for him, and did what I could for him when he got it. He was the only one I knew in the company and I miss him now. He would always have a yarn about when we got a mail.

126

I hope he will make a quick recovery, and get his passage to New Zealand.

I remain

Yours sincerely

Jack Smith

10 Casualty Clearing Station
BEF
22 December 1917

Dear Mr Hawthorne

I am so very sorry to write and tell you that your son 34068 Lance Corporal Hawthorne R. died in this hospital at 1.30 a.m. 21-12-17. He was admitted 20-12-17 badly wounded in his both thighs and left arm. Everything that was possible was done for him. He was quite conscious at first and did not suffer much, he told me to say he had done his bit.

He will be buried in the Military Cemetery Lejssenthock and his personal belongings will be sent to you in due course by the military authorities. Again, saying how very sorry I am for you, in your great trouble.

I remain

Yours faithfully

J H.C. Payther

Sister in Charge

Somewhere in France
21 February 1918

Dear Mr Hawthorne

I am sending you a packet of letters belonging to your late son, Bob. He was wounded in the trenches about the middle of December and it was a great shock to me to hear the other day that he had died, for though he was badly hit, he was conscious throughout and we were all quite hopeful of his recovery. When a man is evacuated from the line he passes from the control of his unit to the medical corps and for that reason it is often hard to trace a wounded man until he writes to his mates from hospital. There are so many hospitals that a man might be sent to, that one can never be sure where he has gone to. Your son was in charge of a Lewis gun section on one of our posts. He was a bright lad, affectionately known to his mates as 'Curly'. It was about 3 p.m. when he was hit. At the time he was lying resting in his bivvy after a night's trying duty, when a shell burst right over the trench and shattered the shelter, severely wounding him on the right arm and left thigh. He was bandaged up and sent back to the dressing station without delay and shook hands with his mates before going. We all felt confident he would pull through. As you know, men take very little personal property up into the trenches and most of his belongings would be in England and will, I expect, be sent to you in the course of time. The letters I am sending you had reached him in the trenches a day or two before he was hit. I remember noticing how pleased he was to get a big mail away up here, and it may comfort you to know he was able to read them. I had been keeping them until I could learn where he was, intending to send them on, but as he has gone, you may like to receive them. Sympathising with you in your bad loss.

I am

Yours truly

L. H. Reeves

2nd Lieutenant

❦

128

Edwin Farrell described what conditions were like on the Somme earlier in this collection. In this letter he describes the experience of being gassed with the new type of gas being used by the Germans on the Western Front. The photo shows New Zealand soldiers inspecting their gas masks after a gas shell bombardment at Bertrancourt, April 1918.

Forest Park Hospital
Brockenhurst
Hants.
28 November 1917

Dear Mother

At last I am in a fit state to write after six weeks of almost total blindness. Two days ago one of the best eye specialists in this country performed an operation on my eyes and removed the fine skin that the gas had caused to envelope both eyeballs and today I can see as well as ever, with the exception that the full light is still too strong after such a long time in complete darkness.

Now I may as well tell you all that has happened to me since my last letter from Camiers base depot.

I left Camiers for the front on the 12 November and proceeded to Hazebrouck where we stopped in the Reinforcement Camp at Morbecque for a few days before going forward to Poperinge, Belgium on the 16 November, where we (me and four other officers) were posted to our different machine gun companies — I being posted to the 4th Company, who were then in the line with their rear headquarters at or about St Jean to the east, or German side, of Ypres. From Poperinge to Ypres was seven miles and we rode it in motor lorries and walked from Ypres to St Jean, where I found my second in command (Captain Geddes) and reported. I stopped there that night and Fritz's planes bombed the camps all night, but did not get any into ours. At midday on the 17th I received orders to go up to the advanced headquarters in a group of pillboxes called the 'Nile', where I found Captain Ingles, our company commander. Another officer, Lieutenant Carswell and a sergeant and six men as reinforcements also went with me.

Captain Ingles told me to take over No. 1 Section and Lieutenant Carswell No. 2 Section, the officers of which had both been gassed. Their names were Lieutenant Williams D.O. and Howden. P. On arrival we made our headquarters together in the same pillbox that Howden and Williams had used. It was a very solid affair untouched by shellfire, but it had one bad fault. It had two openings about 4 foot high and 2 feet wide and both faced Fritz, which meant that a shell was able to be put inside at any moment and if one did explode in such a confined space nobody would escape untouched — if with their lives.

The shell that had gassed Howden and Williams had just hit the left side of the left opening and when we arrived there we found that gas was still inside the pillbox, so we immediately took the usual precautions and soon had the place smelling nice and fresh, after which we visited the gun teams. Carswell and I had two teams each and each had a gun not mounted, in reserve, whose teams lived with us and kept their guns in the pillbox. We found our mounted guns were all serene and laid on SOS lines correctly on direct fire at 2000 yards with our own infantry 1400 yards in front.

Now about the gas.

The shell that had exploded in front of the pillbox was filled with the new mustard oil gas mixed with the deadly phosgene. The mustard gas getting on any portion of the body that is wet, whether with water or perspiration, caused blisters, which in appearance are exactly like burns and are very hard to heal as they turn septic right away. When we returned to the pillbox darkness had descended, so we thought something to eat would be very acceptable, so we . . . all packed inside the pillbox, lit candles and had a good meal, after which we had a game of bridge to help pass the night. About 8 p.m. the gas guard informed us that it was drizzling rain. Then some of the boys began to complain of sore throats and others' eyes began to water. Then some became violently sick and my own eyes and throat became sore and then I too became sick. Mother, I shall never forget that night as long as I live. We all gradually turned blind and sea sickness of the worst kind was a kid's trouble compared to what we suffered — and mind you, Fritz was shelling all around us steadily with 5.9 and 8-inch, trying to break up the abandoned pillboxes.

When daylight came we suffered untold agonies with our eyes, but we collected all the affected men together and with me leading we set out to find our way back. Perhaps to you that sounds easy, but to anybody with all their faculties the Ypres battle sector is a place as easy to lose direction in as the Sahara Desert. I could only see for about two yards in front of me and all the others were in the same plight, with the exception of two who were totally blind and had to be led. I took my direction from my shadow and luckily we did not fall down any holes full of water, although I had hundreds of narrow escapes. At last we hit the duck-walk track that led back, but such a keen wind was blowing that it was almost impossible to see the boards beneath our feet, for our eyes were by this time in an awful state and felt just as though sand had been flung in them.

After a while we hit the headquarters of the 3rd Machine Gun Company and they supplied us with men to help us down to the dressing station at Grief Farm, but when we got there we found that Fritz was doing his best to raze the few remnants of farm buildings with 8-inch shells, so continued our walk to the next dressing station, about two miles further on. The last half-mile I was given a lift in a general's car and from that time I went absolutely blind. I passed through numerous dressing stations to the 3rd Australian Casualty Clearing Station (CCS) and that night was put aboard a hospital train which pulled out at midnight for Rouen, at which city we arrived twenty-four hours later. I do not remember much about that journey, or about anything after reaching the CCS until I wakened up in bed at the 2nd Red Cross Hospital at Rouen. At this place I had wonderful treatment from the nurses and after days I learned that in the room just across the passage from me was Mr Williams, whose place I had taken at the guns. He was in much the same condition as I was, but had pneumonia as a sideline. We were both blind for nine days, but while Mr Williams' sight came back to him without trouble, mine refused to have anything to do with the light, hence my long silence.

I came to England on the 12 November and was sent to this hospital, which is one of the two New Zealand officers hospitals in England. The treatment here is all that can be desired and I am quite contented now that my sight is as good as ever. I will be going out to a convalescent home next Monday and will be there about a week, after which I will be granted two weeks' leave, after which it will be France and hard work again, I suppose.

Now goodbye, with wishes for a prosperous New Year, as I am too late to wish you a Merry Christmas. Love to all at home and my New Year greetings to Mr Henderson and any old friends you may meet. From

Your loving son
Edwin Farrell

Reginald Arthur Calvert (pictured) was wounded on 21 October 1917 near Passchendaele. He returned to New Zealand with an English war bride and was balloted a Returned Services farm. Reginald Calvert had to leave the farm during the Depression years and died in August 1935. This letter is written to his younger brothers.

13 November 1917

Dear Jackie and Lewis

Well, boys, old Fritz has made a hole in me at last. You see, we made a nice new cookhouse, so when Fritz saw it he said, 'Ha! Ha! Now Reggie, I want something to eat,' but I said, 'No Fritz, go away home' so Fritz said, 'I'll go and tell my big brother' and away he went and presently his big brother came along in a plane with a lot of bombs and when he saw the nice new cookhouse he said, 'Now I will spoil that Calvert boy's dinner' so he dropped a bomb and blew the cookhouse over and off Reggie went to hospital in London, so that's all about it.

This is a lovely hospital, boys. There are such nice nurses here from New Zealand, some from Christchurch too, and we get lots and lots of nice things to eat. Cocky would like to be here.

Well, boys, I got your letters in hospital and thank you very much for them. You are both getting on nicely. I hope you are looking after my little dog Piggie.

Goodbye, now, with lots of love and kisses
Your brother
Reg

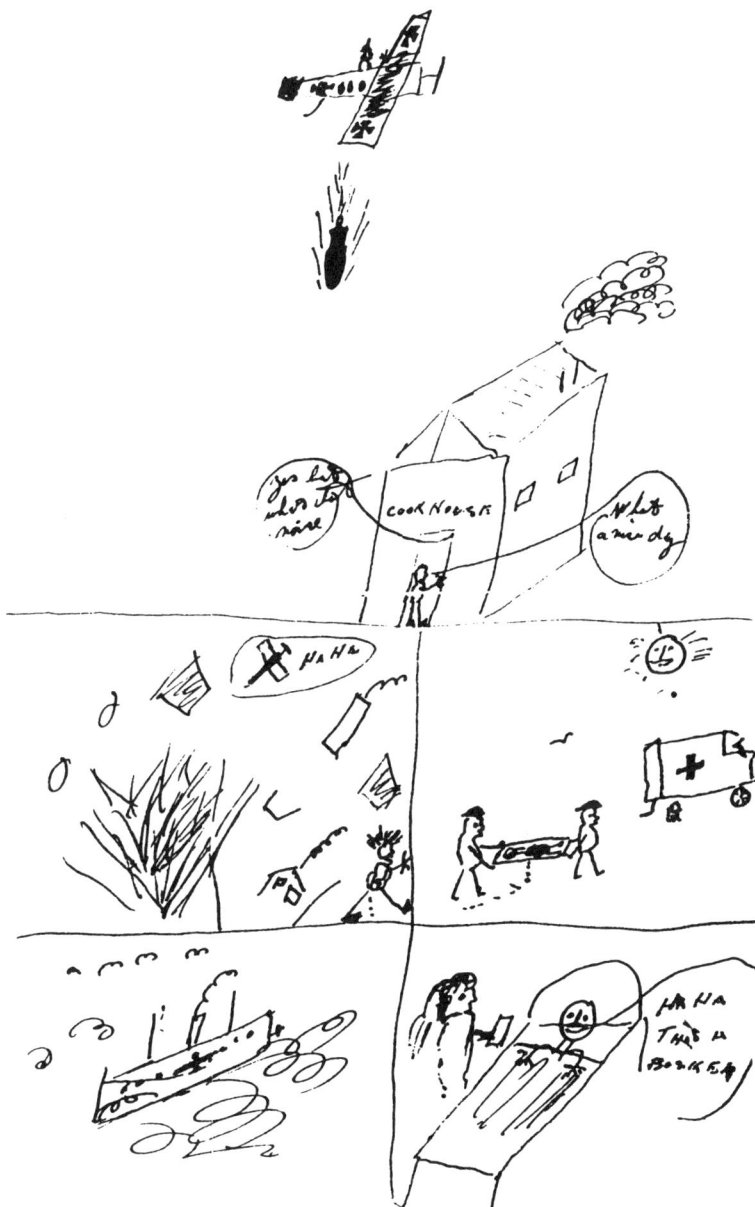

The Western Front
–1918–

The heavy casualties of 1917, combined with a dwindling manpower pool, forced the British to reduce their divisions from 12 infantry battalions to nine at the beginning of 1918. While the Australians soon followed this reorganisation, the Canadians and New Zealanders did not. With its 12 infantry battalions, plus an additional three entrenching battalions formed from the rump of the disbanded 4 New Zealand Brigade, and with an adequate reinforcement pool back in the United Kingdom, the New Zealand Division in 1918 was the strongest division of the British Armies in France. It was, in fact, the equivalent of a British Corps.

The year 1918 was an important one for the Allied divisions on the western front. It was to be the year of victory, yet not one of the warring powers expected the war to end when it did. Certainly General Haig and his staff were planning offensive actions that would carry the war well into 1919. For the New Zealand Division, 1918 began with it recovering from the catastrophic defeat at Passchendaele the previous November. When spring finally arrived the fine weather offered the chance to scrub off the mud and blood of the Ypres salient. The men's spirits and health began to revive.

But it was only the briefest of respites. Towards the end of March came news of a great disaster for the Allied cause. The German Army had launched a massive offensive, the *Kaiserschlacht* or the Kaiser's battle, aimed at winning the war before the armies of the United States joined their allies on the battlefield. The German offensive began well for them and broke the front of an entire British Army. The Fifth Army fell back 20 miles to the Somme, with the Germans hard on their heels. The Germans aimed to take the vital junction town of Amiens, a move that would cut the northern railway system and isolate the Channel ports. To help stem their advance, the New Zealand Division, along with other rested formations, was ordered to entrain for the Somme. Those New Zealanders who had survived the horrors of Passchendaele little imagined that they would soon be playing a crucial role in halting Germany's last attempt to win the war.

The German spring offensive was eventually halted, the result of the stormtroops outrunning their artillery support and logistics chain and then coming up against determined, fresh opposition. With the failure of the offensive there remained little potential for offensive action by the Germans for some time to come. It was now the turn of the Allied armies to strike.

On 8 August 1918, the British Armies in France launched their great offensive that became 'the Hundred Days' that ended the war in France. The Hundred Days was a significant military achievement, prompting the Allied Commander-in-Chief, Marshal Ferdinand Foch, to remark, 'Never in any time in history has the British Army achieved greater results in attack than in this unbroken offensive.' And the New Zealand Division was in the thick of the action.

From August to November 1918 the New Zealand Division, along with the British 37th Division, was almost continuously in action as part of the spearhead of the British Third Army. During this time it never experienced a reverse and came to be regarded as one of the best divisions in France. Morale in the division was high during these months, as the New Zealand soldiers were convinced that they now had the measure of their German opponents. The reasons for the outstanding success of the New Zealand Division during this time were its training, leadership and sheer size. The division also showed an aptitude for open warfare, the soldiers much preferring to be on the move rather than confined to the trenches, where they were at the mercy of enemy artillery and snipers.

There are seven letters in this section, and they cover most of the significant events of 1918. The first letter describes New Zealand's role in halting the German spring offensive in March and April. The next letter details the trench raids that were such a common feature of the New Zealand Division's domination of the sector to which they were allocated. This letter is also significant for its description of the death of Sergeant Dick Travis VC, DCM, MM, Croix de Guerre. Sergeant Travis, 'the King of No-Man's-Land', was the outstanding New Zealand soldier of this war and has reasonable claims to be regarded as New Zealand's greatest soldier. The remaining letters cover the other important events of 1918. These include descriptions of the Hundred Days, of the visit of New Zealand Prime Minister Massey and his deputy to the front, of the outbreak of the influenza pandemic which would kill more people worldwide than the war itself, and of the march of the New Zealand Division in to Germany at the end of the war.

The letters indicate that 1918 was certainly an eventful year for the New Zealand Division. While it was ultimately a successful year for the British and Dominion armies, this success came with a very high price and 1918 was the year these armies experienced their greatest number of casualties. There were 830,000 casualties suffered between March and November 1918, with more than 300,000 casualties in the last three months of the war alone. In 1917, the worst year of the war for the Allies, the casualty figure was 818,000 in total. While New Zealand suffered some 6500 casualties at Messines and a further 7500 for the Passchendaele battles in 1917, their role in halting the German offensive in March and April 1918 cost some 5000 casualties, while the Hundred Days resulted in more than 9000. Winning the war proved an expensive business for all concerned, particularly for those at the forefront of the action, as the New Zealand Division was for most of 1918.

In this letter John Douglas Coleman (pictured) writes to his sister Mary about New Zealand's part in halting the German spring offensive. The last page is missing and may have been censored. John Coleman marched with the Division into Gemany in 1918 and returned to New Zealand the following year. He lived into his 89th year, although his health suffered as a result of his military service.

France
29 April 1918

My Dear Mary

Your two letters written February 18th and 24th have just arrived so I am answering them without delay as we are going into the line tomorrow night, so our mail will then be closed for a few days.

I really forget when I wrote to any of you at Riverside last. I think it was just after I returned to France after my leave. Our company was out in billets for a few weeks' spell, but old Fritz started making things pretty merry, and we were moved away in rather a hurry to quite a different part of the line. We had about eighteen hours' train journey, stayed the night in a village, where we got off the train. Spent most of the night waiting for transport. We made huge fires in the streets and sat around them until I went to sleep, and when I woke up again our fire was out and all the fellows were asleep, huddled up to each other in all sorts of attitudes. Well, we had a good rest in the morning and finally got in the motor lorries at two in the afternoon. We travelled in the lorries for about two hours and then marched about ten miles, where we camped in an open field for the night, but were fortunate enough to get some straw which we nestled in like pigs. There was a fairly hard frost, but we cuddled up close to each other and kept fairly warm.

We marched the next evening to a village that the French had just deserted for the second time, poor beggars. You see some rotten sights on the battlefield, but one is so hardened to them now that you really don't take much notice of what occurs now. All along the road as we came up here we passed continual streams of these poor peasants beating a hasty retreat. This is what touches the soft part of a fellow's heart, to see the poor women and children hurrying along the road with terror-stricken faces. They have all sorts of old-fashioned vehicles moving their happy homes, some with mules drawing them, others horses and some smaller carts drawn by dogs. And what a collection are in some of the carts, furniture, poultry, calves and the cows are generally tied behind like we would lead a horse. Other women might have four or five cows tied coupled together, leading them. Lots of old people, who might be seventy or eighty years old, were wheeling barrows loaded with their goods and chattels. Women, too, and they must have travelled miles.

With all these people retreating in this manner the Huns were steadily advancing. So the little New Zealand division has again made history in this rotten war, I may tell you that there was absolutely no defence on the two-mile front against old Fritz, which we are at present holding. So our boys did not know where the enemy was, one just had to march on until they ran right into them. Then the fight began and our boys must have absolutely cut the Hun to pieces. Our company was supposed to be up here first, but we were delayed on the way. When we went in to hold the lines there were Huns lying dead in all directions.

After we had been there for a couple of days there was a piece of the line wanted straightening, so the boys 'hopped the bags' at two o'clock in the afternoon and caught old Fritz napping. They captured some over a hundred machine guns, 200 prisoners and Lord knows how many were killed, as they were lying about in all directions. Lots of them must have been killed whilst asleep in their bivvys. This was, I think, the most successful little stunt our boys have had, as our casualties were extremely low — small, considering what we gained. We camped just behind the village where these people I speak of had deserted the first night we came up. All the fellows had a pretty gay time as, of course, they ransacked the place, and in lots of the cellars there was champagne and wine galore, so you can imagine all hands had a royal time. Of course, I daren't say where we are, but no doubt you have seen in your papers. It seems rather a sin that this country should be fought over again, as there is so much of it in crops. When we came up here we left our packs behind and just came in battle order, so we have had to sleep in our clothes for the last month. I have had three baths and change of underclothes during that time, so one can't complain.

The last few days we have had a good rest and are at present living in a cellar in an old deserted village and have nothing much to do but eat and sleep. I think if the war goes on much longer a fellow will turn into some strange animal. We must have lived in the trenches when we came up here first for pretty near a month and must have made a dozen different bivvys during that time. When we are making our dugouts it just reminds me of a rabbit or mole making his nest. I am keeping pretty well and so far don't seem to feel any effects of this style of living.

We are getting well into spring again now, all the fruit trees are coming out in blossom and all during the last week I notice the little swallows are coming back to their summer quarters. When I was in the front line the other day I saw our antiaircraft guns bring one of old Fritz's planes down from a good height. By Jove, it was a great sight, he just came down like a corkscrew until about a couple of hundred feet off the ground and then fell like a stone. All I saw afterwards was a cloud of dust. I think we must be much superior in the air now, as we rarely see old Fritz over our lines now, thank goodness too. I shall never forget our experience while we were crouched in almost a water hole at Passchendaele, like cowed rats afraid to move, with old Fritz hovering up and down our line, expecting every minute to get a burst of machine-gun fire on us. I don't think old Fritz can go on making these pushes in massed formation, as his losses must be enormous. It certainly looks as though he is playing his last trump card. I am hoping myself to see America come in with his thousands of aeroplanes.

Kind regards to all.

Much love

J.D. Coleman

⚔

Cecil Bertram Travice McClure (pictured) was a divinity student at Knox Presbyterian College, Otago University in 1914. A year later he volunteered for overseas service as a medical orderly. He later transferred to the Otago Infantry Regiment, where he was commissioned with 10th Company, 2nd Otago Battalion. Lieutenant McClure fought at Messines, Ypres, Passchendaele, Bapaume and Rossignol Wood. Cecil McClure won a Military Cross at

Bellevue Spur on 12 October 1917 and a Bar to the Military Cross at Rossignol Wood in July 1918. In both actions Lieutenant McClure should have won a Victoria Cross, but the New Zealand Commander, General Russell, refused to nominate New Zealand officers for this award. This is a very descriptive letter of life in the trenches in 1918 and is especially significant for its description of the death of Sergeant Travis VC.

Piggaree
Rosignol Farm
31 July 1918

Dear Mother and Father

I have been in some queer places in my time, but never before have I been housed in a pigsty. That is where I am now, however, even with the trough out of which to feed. The weather is perfection just now, but last week the rain was torrential. It has been a momentous week for me as well as for many another, as well as for the Company, which I commanded in the absence of the officer commanding, who was out in rest.

I don't know what news you will be getting of our doings for, after all, they are not much, or indeed of much importance by comparison with the great things of this war. But in our own little world they loom largely, as witness the fact that, as we returned from the funeral of two of our comrades, those who lined the route or occupied billets in the villages through which we passed cheered the boys again and again.

Division has been worrying and worrying the Fritzes opposed to us in such a way as to have him worrying what he was up against. In a captured diary we found the following: 'Opposite us are the English, that is, the New Zealanders of the 42nd Division.' They were well aware later who was troubling them. After our attack and smash up of this counterattack, some American men who were attached showed a lively interest in the prisoners. One, stooping down to a wounded Hun, said, 'You *compris* — United States America?' as he pointed to his badges. '*Nein, nein,*' said Hunny. 'New Zealand, New Zealand.' From this we extracted the fact that no one but the latter would or could give them such a bad time.

It came about this way. Having received several blows and knocks and learning who was responsible through catching one of our boys, he noisily retired from the wood, or in our terms, a very small bush. Noisily, because he blew up all his own dugouts. Quickly summing up the situation, our patrols pushed through and up the various saps and trenches until they came in touch with his posts. Those being all located, our men were soon in line, opposed to them. Owing to the wet and strenuous time the company had had during these few days, we who were in reserve went forward and relieved them. As much to test the opposition as to gain better ground, we received orders to push and occupy certain trenches. Without barrage, beyond a few Stokes mortars . . . we went to it. Bombers and Lewis gunners did the work and in fifteen minutes we had captured and consolidated trenches 500 yards in front and even pushed down the CTs running into Fritz's lines. Only three prisoners were taken, but we accounted for over 100, captured six machine and two pineapple guns, and what must have been hard to Jerry, promptly turned these guns on him.

With his accustomed bravery he turned what artillery he had on to us and began pounding our positions, though with little effect. The next day, towards luncheon hour, he suddenly dropped a regular hailstorm of shells of all shapes and sizes, completely blowing in all the captured trenches and many of the bivvies. It was during this strafe that Division lost its ablest, most capable and most wonderful man — Dick Travis. I have spoken of him before, a man devoid of fear, full of go, of pluck and with an initiative and cunning so far as the Huns were concerned that would have done justice to any Red Indian. He knew the Hun posts after two nights in the trenches. He pinched men whenever they were wanted and was once lost for two days while he surveyed the Huns' reserve lines. A man for whom there was no fitting decoration, who had no equal in his line, the freelance of the army and the only one of the ranks known, not only to all his own Division, but to many others as well. I was talking to some Tommy officers one morning who were taking over from us when seven prisoners passed by. Said a Tommy, 'Is this some more of your mad sergeant's work?' Strangely enough, the same shell killed one of his greatest pals, a man who joined the main body with him and had only been with us a fortnight, having come over from the officer training course at Cambridge.

But to go back, the strafe lasted over an hour and then the dirty Hun went on intermittently till about a quarter to seven, when I think every shell that could fall, and fall without bumping each other, on the space allotted by Fritz and occupied by us, came down. For fifty minutes the storm lasted and then some of his stormtroops broke through our advance post and poured across country to our front lines. On the flanks our chaps simply played havoc with the attackers and none could get within striking distance. Down a deep sap in the centre, however, he overran one post and charged for our line. I shall never forget the result of his mad action. Was it Napoleon who said, 'Two sides will never face each other with the bayonet'? The statement was proved true here. No sooner did our support see what was doing than they up and went to it with the bayonet, and there ensued what might be called a race for our front line, while the posts in the line itself poured lead into the charging enemy. As suddenly, almost, as the contest began, it dwindled away. And as if on the instructional ground, the Huns came through our troops running on, but with hands well aloft and yelling beseechingly, 'Kamerad, kamerad.'

In less than half an hour, our whole line was re-established and only the wreck and debris of the attack showed that anything unusual had taken place. I promised my battalion at least fifty prisoners, but only twenty reached them. Intelligence says, 'The others were killed by their own shell fire, which continued rather heavily on our support line.' Our casualties during the attack itself were slight, but here again we lost another of our best officers and the knowledge of this, I'm afraid, was hardly conducive to the taking of many prisoners.

Later we were relieved and I came out with the Company to hand them over to the officer commanding with much fear and trembling, but he himself had gone to hospital sick and so, of the officers, I alone was left. One of the officers wounded was Dobbie, whose father was stationmaster at Woodville once. He was exploiting success by taking the Hun as one might chase rabbits when a Kamerad Hun got him in the back with a bomb. The officer killed, Beechy, had been wounded in the advance post and the charging Huns had bayoneted him. Can mercy in such cases be tempered with justice?

And now there are, posted to the Company, two officers who were sergeants in the same reinforcement with me. I had hoped it would be my turn for a rest out back this time, but it is not to be, though later I go to a rest house near the seaside for a week. Ought to be some good this time of the year, don't you think? Fancy the seaside in France in the summer!

Brigade, Division, Corps and Army have all sent for reports of our successful repulse of the counterattack and the Army Commander has

142

issued a special order of thanks to the New Zealand Division on its most successful work. All the bigwigs are as pleased as punch about the whole show too, and so it is needless to say our old tin hats fit us much better now than prior to the stunt.

Here is a copy of the order:

> 'GOC Fourth Army Corps.
> The repulse of the enemy raid with such heavy loss to the raiders reflects the greatest credit on all ranks of the garrison. The initiative shown by the leaders and men in rallying and surrounding those of the enemy who had entered our line at Slug Street is an object lesson in readiness and resource.
> (Signed) J. Byng, General
> 3rd Army.

We are living in luxury now with cricket matches, concerts and entertainments every day. Baths in plenty and *beaucoup* vegetables for the men, cases of tomatoes being also sent up from the south of France. By the way, one man, being carried out with two of his toes off, says laughingly, 'By crumbs, I got it on to that old toe this time. That's the old beggar that gave me all the trouble on route marches.' The night we were relieved, some Yanks came in with our troops and two of them were slightly wounded. They went off to the regiment aid post with another chap on a stretcher. The doctor said, 'Righto, go down below and I'll see you when I get the stretcher case fixed.' Said they, 'Say guy, we're not stopping here tonight. We want to go right on. We guess we'll die a natural death rather than be caught here.'

With love to you both,
From
Cecil

∞

Private J.M. Nimmo (pictured, centre back) of the New Zealand Rifle Brigade wrote many letters home to his family. Part of one of these letters, describing New Zealand's role in the Hundred Days, follows.

An Ex Fritz Dugout
30 September 1918

Dear Mother and all at home

Just a few lines to let you know everything is going first rate over here. We have been gradually working up towards the front line, but old Fritz is going so hard that I'm afraid we will have to get a motorcar to catch up on him. He is leaving munitions galore, and prisoners are being taken in thousands. We must have passed 1000 of them yesterday, and they were looking as pleased as punch with themselves. They are mighty glad to be prisoners. From all appearances Fritz is done, absolutely. Only about two Fritz aeroplanes appeared all day yesterday, and they weren't in sight for more than five minutes. On the other hand, hundreds of ours were going about all day. Our observation balloons were up all day, his weren't allowed to stop up for any length of time at all. He is outclassed in artillery by about six to one, so the old hands tell us. From what we can see from here it appears as if we have an even greater superiority than that. He was chucking a few shells in this vicinity yesterday.

So far this war hasn't been nearly so bad as I expected. The shells make you jump at first, but you soon get used to them.

✂

144

Private William Malcolm (pictured left), from Enfield near Oamaru, enlisted with his brother George for service overseas. Sadly, 2nd Lieutenant George Malcolm of the Rifle Brigade was killed on the Somme in 1918, only three hours into his first day on the battlefield. There are three letters here, two written by William Malcolm, the other by Jack Hinton, pictured far right with his close friend, George Malcolm.

France
12 June 1918

Dear Mum

I'm sorry to have left writing to you alone these past few days, but as I told you before, I wanted to find George's grave and then let you know. Well, today I went up and put a cross on it.

I had the map reference to the grave from Jack Hinton, so went to the YMCA secretary, Mr Horner, and borrowed his map. He was good enough to go up with me. On the way we picked up an Otago padre, who came up with us as well. The place marked on the map was just behind the line on ground I had searched before . . . but we had no luck . . . Next day I scored leave to find the 4th Battalion . . . There I met a Sergeant Sutherland, who was with George at the time [of his death].

Their platoon was in a very awkward position and George, who was in command, was keen on a bombing stunt against Fritz. He asked for volunteers, so Sutherland and seven others went out with him just a little after stand-to on the morning of the 28th. They got well on to the Hun with bombs. In one place he had raised a white flag as well as the Red Cross, so they left that alone.

Sutherland said that they had the Germans so much frightened that they all jumped out on top in such numbers that they could have rushed George's party empty handed. He said he had never seen so many Huns with their hands up before. I know from the number of dead that lay there when we went up, how many they were up against. The trench was a fearful sight. George's party were in a position that they could not possibly take them prisoner.

The trouble was that they had no support, so they retired, sniping all the time. George was firing from behind cover, as cool as could be, when Fritz opened up with a machine gun from the Red Cross possie, which seems to have been on their flank. His first burst caught George and another chap . . . Sutherland said George must have died instantly. The bodies lay for a day till the advance was made, when they were all buried. The padre who read the burial service has since been killed. George was buried beside Sergeant Jamieson and a little cross was put up, but it must have been knocked down by flying pieces of shell . . .

Mr Horner spoke to the pioneer sergeant of his battalion, who agreed to make a cross for me to put up. I got it yesterday so I asked the officer commanding for leave to go up and erect it this morning. It may not be over the exact spot, but it cannot be more than a foot or two out of place . . . Mr Horner says I can have a photo of it taken to send home to you, if I write to London, so I will do so. I did not forget to say a prayer, as you would all have done if you were able to stand by his grave. A boy such as he was does not die . . .

I hope you are all well.

Your loving son,

Willie

New Zealand Convalescent Home
4 Lewes Crescent
Brighton
10 April 1918

Dear Mrs Malcolm

This morning the sad news reached here about George and I feel I must drop you a line.

He and I entered camp together and spent much of our time together. Especially was this so after we got our commissions, for on all our leave we had each other's company. On the steamer we were inseparable — in fact it seems for the last year, all our work was done together, all our pleasure was taken together, and with the optimism of youth we had planned our course for after the war . . .

He knew my every thought and plan and I knew his and so I can speak of his worth. In nothing have I found him unworthy. How I will miss his friendship! His advice I have become accustomed to seek in everything, so I mourn his loss very deeply indeed.

I started off to ask you not to mourn too deeply, and I have only expressed my own grief. But really I know how little he feared death and that he himself would desire that we mourn not, but rather be glad that he has gained eternal rest. I say in absolutely all sincerity that he had absolutely no vices and his reward is assured.

In your natural grief I tender you all my deepest sympathy, but again I ask you to regard this as he did — a very temporary parting. Would that I could have kept him company even to the end!

Please excuse the rambling nature of this note. I hope to see some of the other officers in London this week and learn more details. I will write you more calmly then.

Meanwhile I will close by again expressing my very great sympathy.

Yours sincerely

J.W. Hinton

P.S. I hope to go to France in a fortnight and will endeavour to see Bill.

41975 2nd Lieutenant J.W. Hinton

France
7 July 1918

Dear Sis [*Margaret*]

I have been rather long in answering to your letter this time. At present I am up in the line again.

Since I last wrote I have had the pleasure of staring at Bill and Joe [Massey and Ward]. They came along last Sunday morning to church parade, which was attended by all the tin hats. Pretty well all the brigade was on parade and we were jumping to attention while they approached, but that did not prevent some digger from roaring out, 'Good morning, Bill.' We did not get much of a chance to barrack them.

When the service was over the two old boys were trotted up and down the ranks of each battalion. They both looked as uncomfortable as fish out of water. Of course, we were treated to the usual little speech. Bill advised us to get on with the war and he hoped we would soon be on the road to New Zealand again. Cheering, wasn't he? Joe followed with one equally as short.

They are both getting the worse for wear. Bill seems much older, while the pleasures of London life seem to be telling on Sir Joe. They had been at a concert among the Dinks the night before. No doubt when they get home you will hear some yarns as to how they escaped from bombs and shells. Fritz did give them one or two of each.

I went down to see Gordon Cummins that night and found him down with the Spanish fever [influenza] which has a great hold in the division. Chaps are still going down with it, but I'm blowed if I can catch it! We have had to do eight days in the front line as the other battalions were too weak to relieve us . . . I am acting No. 2 at present. The real No. 2 is down with the flu. Poor Gordon was the picture of misery the evening I saw him, but he will be back at work now . . .

11th July. We were relieved in fairly good time from the outpost by some of the 2nd Brigade . . . While we were in the front line the next platoon sent out its usual patrol. This night the corporal in charge went a little too far and was crossing over a fence when he was challenged by a Fritz sentry. He is a fairly cool customer, but I guess he had the wind up while he took his legs out of the wire. A bomb is a nasty little affair once the pin is out!

One chap in our platoon had a bullet right through his arm. Such a lovely one, and he had the cheek to say, 'Hard luck, boys'. Needless to say, no one sympathised with him. No. 2 on one of our guns got hit with shrapnel on his boot and went his way down the trench rejoicing and hoping that it had managed to break a bone. The strangest thing about it all is that everyone wants a Blighty, but when a bit of iron is flying through the air all hands duck . . .

At night the New Zealand mail arrived with ten letters, two *Witnesses* and that pair of socks for me . . . An *Otago Witness* is as common as an *Auckland Weekly* with this company now . . . I had a letter from Donald last night telling me of his fat cheque, but he is a big mug if he goes on the [chaff] cutter. DM, you will learn yet what a good job is so take my advice and don't run from home, even if Bill Massey offers you one . . .

I will have to cut this short, Sis.

Best of love to you all.

Bill

✄

James McKenzie (pictured), a private in the 1st Auckland Infantry Battalion, was a farmer from Okaihou in the Bay of Islands. This letter was written to Alice White, the 'girl next door' whom Jim McKenzie married shortly after his return from the war. This letter is used with permission of the Hughes family.

149

Rue Berthelot, Billet 163
Beauvois, France
23 November 1918

Dear Alice

I received your letter of September 8th a week or so ago and was very pleased to hear from you again. Now you can get out your map and find out where we are, as censorship has ceased. You may find this town, it is a bit to the southeast of Cambrai.

Soon we are expecting to be moving up to Germany, some travellers we, eh? We are in pretty comfortable quarters here, Alice. At the present time I am sitting by a stove with a good fire, four of us in one room. It is fairly cold here now, plenty of frost, but only a slight fall of snow yet, we are getting beautiful clear weather now, no rain for weeks.

Well, Alice, I guess you must be all greatly relieved now the war is over. I thought at one time when peace came we would all go mad-like, but strange to say, when the news came through the boys took it very quietly, and there was practically no demonstration.

It took us quite a while to realize that it was all over, and that we would go over the top no more, but we are just beginning to believe it now.

Fancy, no more shells, no more bullets, no more sleeping in dirty wet trenches etc., etc. I was about on the verge of tears, thinking of putting in another winter on the line, and I sometimes used to wish I'd get a smack to get out for a while, but my luck was out. I could not even get a decent headache. However, I suppose a whole skin is the best after all.

This village or town we are in is just the usual French town, they are all pretty much the same, just a few dirty streets and brick houses of pretty much the same pattern. This one would probably have had a population of six or seven thousand.

Since hostilities ceased the people are coming back in good numbers every day, old men and women, and children of all ages, each carrying a bundle of some sort, all their worldly possessions. I had a look through the church here a few days ago and it was simply lovely inside, beautiful carving etc., but Fritz, before he retired from town, had put a mine under the front door to blow it up, but it had only blown the doorway out and cracked the walls a bit. By Jove, my blood fairly boiled when I went in and saw what a beautiful place the dirty dogs had tried to destroy.

In some other town we passed through I have seen the church left a heap of bricks and masonry, that's German Kulture for you.

I sent you a Christmas card, Alice and I hope it reaches you in good time. I had just returned from Blighty leave, where I had a very good time. I made some very good friends over there and they treated me real well, and I think, 'Little Shimmy', he cry when he come back to France.

Yes, Alice, I don't mind giving you a few hints on cooking, if you don't let on to anyone. I'll give you a recipe for making a stew. Of course, we never have anything but stew and tea to make here, barring accidents such as accidentally getting oatmeal, of which we would then make burgoo [porridge]. If you call at my home in New Zealand they will give you my favourite burgoo recipe which I left there, on the piano. I suppose it is still there unless it got knocked off. You might kindly ask them at home if they have shifted my boots that I left by the doorstep on the verandah. I left a pair of socks on the floor alongside the boots. I hope they haven't shifted them as I do hate having my things shifted — I never know where to find them.

I say, Alice, you might ring Bill up and ask him about these things and by Jove, now I come to think of it I left my saddle and bridle on the fence, near the orange tree. Ask Bill if he'll take them in, I forgot to mention it to him before, as they might get wet if they are left there any longer. Of course, if it is too much trouble tell him not to bother.

By Jove, Alice, tell him I left some soap in the creek where I used to swim. Ask him if he'll go and take it out, or it might waste away before I return. Tell your dad too, Alice, that I saw two of his sheep stuck in a slip up near the sheep yards. I was going to mention it to him before I came away, but forgot. Tell him he had better go up before it is too late and pull them out, besides it is not too comfortable for them there. Well, now, the recipe for stew, mind this is strictly confidential.

Take in a dixie full of water, then take it out again and empty a third in a dish for washing up, then place the dixie on a hot fire, as a cold one has been proved to be a failure. When the water has boiled put in anything and everything you can get hold of, biscuits (Anzac Wafers) potato peelings, grease of any sort, if no vegetables are procurable, a few chips or splinters of wood help to give it the vegetable flavour necessary. No cigarette butts or boot laces or rags should be put in, as by experience they have been found unnecessary.

After boiling for three hours you will find that you have forgotten to put the bully beef in, so you swear aloud and for at least five minutes, but as this does not seem to thicken the stew you call it soup, and in serving up, strive to give each one a spot of grease and a chip of wood.

Well, Alice, so much for that. Now I guess I'll have to close and write some of my other letters I owe. I had a letter from Marshall a few days ago, he is still in Blighty, lucky beggar. I guess he won't come over here again. Now, dear Alice, will say *au revoir* hoping to see you all before those peaches are all done. Kindest regards to all.

Yours sincerely

Jim McKenzie

Epilogue:
The Great War: Needless or Necessary?
A Historian's Journey

For as long as I can remember I have been fascinated by the events of 1914–18. I think many New Zealanders share this fascination, as well as a strong desire to know more about the Great War. My views on the war have changed significantly since I first started reading about it as a schoolboy growing up in New Zealand during the 1970s. This is especially true about two aspects of the First World War; that is, its necessity and the performance of the senior military commanders throughout the war.

At high school we had to read as a class text Erich Remarque's evocative *All Quiet on the Western Front*. This book, the classic anti-war novel, so moved me that I followed it up by reading its sequel, *The Road Back*. After reading both books I felt that the Germans were not such bad people after all. They had certainly suffered as much as any people involved in a war, which had started through some kind of terrible accident. The Great War had made victims of us all for no purpose. It seemed, too, that no single person or country was responsible for causing it. At school, the reading of Remarque was followed by a liberal dose of the poets of this war, especially the poems of Siegfried Sassoon and Wilfred Owen. The reading of the war poets soon became a yearly ritual around Anzac Day. Little wonder that I soon formed the opinion, along with many of my classmates, that the war had been futile and the men on both sides had merely been 'lambs to the slaughter'. The generals who had fought the war I regarded as incompetent, vain, and foolhardy. They also seemed callous and uncaring and I regarded them as little better than war criminals.

The first book on the Great War I bought after leaving school confirmed these views. It was A.J.P. Taylor's best seller, *The First World War: An Illustrated History*, first published in 1963. I still have this book, although its binding has long since given way. It's held together now by a rubber band. *The First World War: An Illustrated History* still impresses with the clarity of its prose, its breadth and with its uncompromising condemnation of the high command on both sides. Professor Taylor's view of the war can be summed up in one line from this brilliant but misleading history: 'brave helpless soldiers; blundering obstinate generals; nothing achieved'. For most of my early life this was how I regarded the war. It is, I suspect, how many of my generation view the war still.

It wasn't until my third year as a history student at university that I was able to study the First World War. Even then, the one paper where the Great War featured only examined the war's causes and the Treaty of Versailles that ended it. The whole war experience was ignored, as it still is in most New Zealand universities today. But even this was enough to cause me to rethink some of my earlier views. One of the texts to which we were introduced was Fritz Fischer's *Germany's Aims in the First World War*. This groundbreaking work by a German professor of history showed conclusively that Germany in 1914 aimed at a war of conquest and expansion that would give Germany dominance over most of Europe and much of the world. While many historians disputed Fischer's claims and tried to discredit them, they failed to do so. Other historians, most notably Immanuel Geiss, Paul Kennedy and Volker Berghahn, have built on Fischer's pioneering efforts and have concluded, like Fischer, that Germany in 1914 embarked on a war of aggressive expansion designed to transform Germany into the dominant European and world power.

The works of two Australian historians, John Moses and Jurgen Tampke, also support this view. For the best part of twenty years, Professor John Moses has argued that Germany's aggressive expansion extended well in to the South Pacific. Far from being a war forced upon them by manipulative masters in London, the First World War was very much Australia (and New Zealand's) war too. This view is supported and developed by Associate Professor Jurgen Tampke of the University of New South Wales, who in a recent publication entitled *'Ruthless Warfare'. German military planning and surveillance in the Australia-New Zealand region before the Great War*, concluded that both Australia and New Zealand were regarded as legitimate targets of opportunity by the German military. The German navy planned (and several of the planning documents are presented in the book) to wage 'ruthless warfare' against Australian and New Zealand harbours. In doing so they planned to inflict as much damage as possible, including the killing of citizens in Australia and New Zealand and the taking by force of any natural resources such as coal and wood.

The Great War then, for the writers mentioned above, was not only New Zealand and Australia's war, but had a purpose, even a noble purpose, similar to the war of 1939–45.

Certainly the New Zealand soldiers fighting in this war and whose letters are recorded here did not see the war as an exercise in futility. While the war dragged on and was unnecessarily costly in their eyes, they were well aware of what they were fighting for. As the concluding letter in this collection, states: 'Whilst still in the happy world, for it is a happy world and I have found it so, when this affair is over, you may be better assured that we have been part contributors to the general good of mankind and as such, I hope you may live to enjoy it.' This letter was written as a final testament and the convictions expressed in it are deeply held. As one of the relatives who submitted letters for this collection and who lost two uncles in France wrote to me recently: 'The one fact that shone out of all the letters home was the absolute belief in what they were fighting for — King and Country and their loved families back home.' It may be that only the subsequent generations of New Zealanders have lost sight of this purpose.

The notion that the high commanders of the war, particularly British and French commanders, were nothing but 'Butchers and Bunglers' has also been challenged recently. In works by Tim Travers, by the Australian historians Robin Prior and Trevor Wilson, and by Paddy Griffith, these authors have traced a clear and continuous tactical learning curve for commanders at all levels. They have also traced a great willingness to embrace new technology and techniques that would give any advantage on the battlefield. It would appear then that the British officer corps was not the unthinking, unresponsive, stagnant entity that it has so often been portrayed as. Those who describe the British methods during 1914–18 as being based solely on unthinking obedience, draconian military law and limited intellectual capabilities, ignore much of the evidence to the contrary. As Trevor Wilson and Robin Prior have noted of this conflict:

> The emergence of the industrial economy, and the application of industrial technology to the battlefield, ensured that

for any participant this war was going to prove a terrible killing experience. We need only notice the 1.8 million slain of
Germany, or the 1.7 million of Russia, or the 1.4 million of
France, to appreciate that 'silly British Generals' is not an all
encompassing explanation of Britain's lost generation of
700,000.

This, then, is where I have reached in my historical journey on the
First World War on these two issues. My journey is by no means over
and there are many other issues to consider too. But for me, the First
World War was not futile and unnecessary. It was fought to prevent an
aggressive, militarist nation from achieving dominance over other nations by force. In fighting against the aggressors and in defence of lesser
nations, the war was every bit as noble and just as the war that followed it twenty years later. And far from being unthinking, uncaring
automatons (and there were some of these) the military commanders
of this war had many military problems to overcome in the face of the
new technologies being applied on the battlefield. In response, most
of them tried to learn how to achieve victory in these new circumstances as quickly as they knew how, but it was a slow, costly process.
Beginning in 1917 and by the end of the war, the Allies adopted an all-
arms approach on the battlefield and used their advantage in the air to
inflict severe defeats on the German army, forcing it back many miles.
By the middle of 1918 the Allies had finally discovered a formula for
achieving success in the conditions then prevailing on the Western Front
and they demonstrated this conclusively during the Hundred Days.
The Germans, exhausted after four years of war and blockade, and
with no answers to the Allied onslaught that occurred from August
1918, requested an armistice three months later.

The above quote by Prior and Wilson emphasises another important point. While the notion of the futility of the Great War and the
incompetent, blundering generals is part of the mythology that sur-
rounds it, the extent of the casualties is not. Prior and Wilson are right.
This war proved to be a terrible killing experience for all nations involved in it, New Zealand included. The cost of fighting for King,
country and families in 1914–18 to preserve the rights and freedoms
we now take for granted was many dead and damaged New Zealanders. The final three letters here remind us of the price this nation paid
for its involvement in the most important and deadly conflict of the
twentieth century.

This letter is to Mrs Juliett Christophers. It describes for her the details of the gravesite of Julian Christophers (pictured), one of her four sons killed in the war. Julian Christophers was the brother of Victor Christophers, whose letters appear on pages 36–39 of this book.

Berlin
Germany
29 June 1930

Dear Mrs Christophers

    When Doctor and I were staying at Ypres in Belgium — we were one day visiting some of the cemeteries at Poperinge of our boys' graves, and we came across one of Julian Anthony Christophers 45990 26-3-17. So we thought he must have been one of your sons who was buried there. It made us feel so sad, seeing the rows and rows of graves from the war. But all these sacred places are so splendidly set out and so well kept that in a way it was a beautiful thing to see. For not even their own could do more for them, nor honour them more than where they rest. We met a gardener who is English, and who has been working in charge of one of these war cemeteries for years and we had a long talk to him. Your son's grave had some blue violas blooming upon it and so I picked three of them to send you. I have to enclose this in with Mrs Petrie's letter, which that good soul will see that you get . . . as I cannot think of your address. Doctor and I are having a very wonderful trip, full of interesting wonders and have now been on the continent for six weeks. You will have heard that we left Shirley at school in England, I suppose. I did not like parting from her, but it had to be done as she could not miss so much schooling. Mrs Petrie tells me you have not been very well and we were sorry to hear that — are you still playing plenty of games of bridge? Well, I must stop as it is very late. Doctor's regards to you and with love from

Yours sincerely

Elsie

✂

This is the last letter written by Sergeant Allan Wilson (pictured) of the 2nd Auckland Infantry Battalion of the Auckland Infantry Regiment. Sergeant Wilson was killed on 4 October 1917 in the first New Zealand attack at Passchendaele. This letter, his last testament to his family, was found in his pocket after he had been killed.

France
In the Pas de Calais
Good Friday, 1917

My Dear Father

If ever you read these lines, you will be aware that I have been called upon to render the most extreme sacrifice that my country can ask of her sons.

At the time of writing, I am living behind the lines in France, about 17 miles from the front. I have not yet been under fire, but expect at anytime to be ordered forward in the biggest offensive movement so far contemplated by our side.

What my sensations may be or how I shall comport myself, I can only leave for the present as a futile discussion.

I am, however, sensitive of the extreme possibility of a hit of some description being encountered.

There has been much said of the terrible selfishness of the battlefield: an extremely real presentiment of the occasional preeminence of the first law of nature.

My prayer now, is that I be relieved from allegiance to this law.

It is the human failing which is justly, no doubt, termed cowardice.

No one is quite free from these terrible struggles with self, and I can only earnestly record my determination to play the game.

I cannot make this last message a bulky one, but I should like to touch on the theme to which most people turn in such times as these.

I am afraid my sentiments about religion are too chaotic to be easily defined, but broadly speaking, my attitude is based on self-reasoning, which is at times, coincident with and sometimes repugnant to the doctrine of the church.

I have had ample opportunity of receiving the sacrament, but have consistently refrained from a profession of faith, which, in fact, I did not and could not, in all sincerity, adopt.

I cannot regard the matter of religion as a thing ready made and suitable for blind, unconditional acceptance by all.

I know the spirit of Christ's teachings fulfills my idea of right living, although I fail to find an application of it practical enough for universal use today.

The older part of the Bible, wherein I feel there are many fables I have been unable to find the guidance or the tangible evidence of the hereafter spoken of, which every Christian holds as a sacred and indispensable pillar of his faith.

I have known so many good people, amongst whom I count yourself, Grandpa and Grandma, who have lived this life not without mistakes, but with a genuine trend for good, and have been so adversely situated for the greater part of it that I believe a well-ordered universe like ours cannot fail to make provisions for recompense in this, as it does in all other directions, the consciousness of self demands something higher in the matter of reward or retribution than is possible on Earth.

The emotion of hope seems in itself to justify some elevation, the faculty of feeling for other separate beings sets a line between the attitude of one man to another, as against one dog to another, more than this, I fear, I cannot profess. The Bible (or at least the older portion) is not without foundation, I think, has been ascribed in part, at least, to the myths of hundreds of generations of men. Myths which become distorted and changed not only in form, but in becoming truths and beliefs in place of their original existence as hopes and desires.

I cannot profess the Christian faith in its entirety, but I agree with its ordering of a man's life. I cannot accept unreservedly the promise of the hereafter, although I see no reason why it should not be, and have all a human's desire that it should be.

I might say as Nelson said, that I have not been a great sinner. I am not intimately acquainted with the history of his environment, but I do not recall that he had any special scope in the direction of sinning badly.

Summarily, myself, I have had nothing to gain by blinding myself to my failings and I have often had cause to congratulate myself that my surroundings were conducive to restraining the natural impulses.

I have, therefore, to consider how little opportunity I have had for transgression of the laws to any extent before I quit my barque.

I have always been conscious of a peculiar temperament which has prevented me in a great part from partaking in the social pleasures of my own acquaintances. That this was no acquired characteristic, I am satisfied, for I have had the most pronounced tastes in the matter of companionship since the first day I went to school, it has continued ever since.

I have had ambitions and I have dreamed. I am conscious of a supersensitive nature in my own way.

I have been the recipient of many a jeer from my everyday associates.

I have been active from choice, but not necessarily in acquiring that which might be of use to me in earning my bread. I have read whatever I could manage to get hold of in the way of scientific works.

I have dabbled in electricity, theology and accounting. I have repaired boots, learned to cook and play the handyman from a natural desire ever present in me to be acquainted with the ordinary problems of life. The point is (and I do not know why, mind you) that I have never possessed an unsatiable desire to acquire information which has, through my temperament, never been confined to a speciality, so have held forth prospects of succession in life, unless it has happened that a radical change had taken effect.

And now, dear Father, I close this last message. I leave the remainder of our little family intact so far as I know.

We were scattered sooner than most families of a standing compatible with your position. To each and all of you, Mother, Brothers and Sisters, I address myself and desire for you all that prosperity and long life, that fate may hold in store for you. Look to one another, and do not above all things, become strangers.

Whilst still in the happy world, for it is a happy world and I have found it so, when this affair is over, you may be better assured that we have been part contributors to the general good of mankind and as such, I hope you may live to enjoy it. My affairs as I have indicated, are in Aunt Nellie's hands and she will communicate to you, no doubt, the essence of the Will, which I left with her.

To her, by the way and Uncle and the boys (Bertram and Horace), I owe much.

Goodbye and remember that my greatest regret is in leaving this existence without seeing you all again.

Your ever affectionate and dutiful son,

Allan

✄

The following extract is taken from Jim Henderson's Soldier Country. *It was written by W.G. Hulse of Cambridge and is used by permission of Jim Henderson (Gunner 24563). The above photo was taken near Bertrincourt, France.*

The night is black as men grope their way, and their horses' way, back to the picket line, lighted only by an occasional feeble torch.

'Feed!'

Nosebags are adjusted, and the poor old neddies set to, gratefully champing their suppers.

There is no cooked meal for us either! Hard biscuits, and bully beef reduced to oily string through tossing about in haversacks in the heat of the day. To drink, water — brackish — from the well. By 8.45, with line-guards posted, outlying pickets (poor sods!) set out in front and on flanks, the Squadron's men stretch out their weary bones behind the horse-lines, and ease puttees and boots. Roll in blankets, a last puff at a cigarette, which is carefully pinched out and saved, and settle down to sleep.

About 9.30 a peeping half-moon creeps over the horizon, to show what looks like a camp of the dead, men and horses stretched out sleeping the sleep of exhaustion.

Sleep well — reveille is at 3 a.m.

When daylight came the Turks had gone. W.G. Hulse was told they had retired to a new line defending Beersheba.

We scrambled down to our horses, watered and fed them, washed a week's grime off ourselves, shaved. And a glorious feeling it was!

We led our horses up on the plain where a crop of barley was just long enough for the horses to nibble.

Claud Hill and I lay on our backs looking up into a beautiful blue sky. A skylark sang overhead, poppies, with stems so slender they were hardly visible, swayed in a gentle breeze like crimson butterflies. Big guns away in the distance near Gaza kept up a constant rumble, but here we were at peace.

Claud turned to me and said: 'I wonder if we were killed last night, and this is heaven?'

Claud was killed when the Turks counterattacked at the Wadi Adju just north of Jaffa.

Are the skies blue where you are Claud? Are the skylarks singing and the poppies swaying in the breeze?

Endnotes

1. Jay Winter and Blaine Baggett, *1914–18. The Great War and the Shaping of the 20th Century*, BBC Books, London, 1996, p. 361.
2. Winter and Baggett, p. 11.
3. Niall Ferguson, *The Pity of War*, Penguin, London, 1998, p. 434.
4. Ferguson, p. 435.
5. Peter Simkins, 'Everyman at War: Recent Interpretations of the Front Line Experience' in Brian Bond (ed) *The First World War and British Military History*, Clarendon Press, Oxford, p. 309.
6. There is considerable confusion over the New Zealand casualty rate and how it compares to that of the other combatants. Simkins, p. 309 and Jeffrey Grey, *A Military History of Australia*, Cambridge University Press, Melbourne, 1999, p. 115, claim that New Zealand's per capita casualty rate was the highest of the war. Ferguson p. 299 and Jay Winter, *The Great War and the British People*, London, 1985, p. 75 dispute this. They give New Zealand's per capita casualty rate as 1.5 per cent and list several other countries whose rate is higher than this (Turkey 3.7 per cent, Germany 3.0, France 3.4). It would appear that Serbia at 5.7 per cent holds the dubious distinction of the highest number of casualties as a percentage of its population.
7. Bill Folwler, quoted in Lyn Macdonald *They Called it Passchendaele. The story of the Third Battle of Ypres and of the men who fought in it*, Penguin, London, 1978, p. xiii.
8. Winter and Baggett, p. 15.
9. Christopher Pugsley, *On the Fringe of Hell. New Zealanders and Military Discipline in the First World War*, Hodder and Stoughton, Auckland, 1991, p. 9.
10. Bill Gammage, *The Broken Years. Australian Soldiers in the Great War*, Penguin, Melbourne, 1974, p. 277.
11. John Keegan, *The First World War*, Hutchinson, London, 1998, p. 262.
12. Grey, p. 3.
13. Quoted in Gammage, p.279.

Select Bibliography

Bond, Brian (ed) *The First World War and British Military History*, Clarendon Press, Oxford, 1991.

Ferguson, Niall *The Pity of War*, Penguin, London, 1998.

Gammage, Bill *The Broken Years. Australian soldiers in the Great War*, Penguin, Melbourne, 1974.

Grey, Jeffrey *A Military History of Australia*, Cambridge University Press, Melbourne, 1999.

Griffith, Paddy *Battle Tactics of the Western Front. The British Army's Art of Attack 1916–18*, Yale University Press, London, 1994.

Keegan, John *The First World War*, Hutchinson, London, 1998.

Macdonald, Lyn *They Called it Passchendaele. The story of the Third Battle of Ypres and of the men who fought in it*, Penguin, London, 1978.

Moses, John A. *The Terror of Naivety and the Arrogance of Orthodoxy: Australian Historians and the First World War*, UNE Union, Armidale, 1999.

Moses, John A. with Munro, Gregory *Australia and the 'Kaiser's War' 1914–1918. On Understanding the ANZAC Tradition. Argument and Thesis*, Broughton Press, Brisbane, 1993.

Prior, Robin and Wilson, Trevor *Command on the Western Front: The Military Career of Sir Henry Rawlinson 1914–18*, Blackwell, Oxford, 1992.

Prior, Robin and Wilson, Trevor 'During the Great War, Great Britain lost over 700,000 lives in battle. Was this sacrifice necessary?' in Wilcox, Craig and Aldridge, Janice (eds) *The Great War. Gains and Losses ANZAC and Empire*, Australian War Memorial and the Australian National University, Canberra, 1995.

Pugsley, Christopher *On the Fringe of Hell. New Zealanders and military discipline in the First World War*, Hodder and Stoughton, Auckland, 1991.

Travers, Tim *How the War Was Won: Command and Technology in the British Army on the Western Front 1917–1918*, Routledge, London, 1992.

Winter, Jay *The Great War and the British People*, London, 1985.

Winter, Jay and Baggett, Blaine *1914–18. The Great War and the Shaping of the 20th Century*, BBC Books, London, 1996.

Index